The Killer Preacher

Danny Curry

Published by Trellis Publishing, 2021.

While every precaution has been taken in the preparation of this book, the publisher assumes no responsibility for errors or omissions, or for damages resulting from the use of the information contained herein.

THE KILLER PREACHER

First edition. July 11, 2021.

Copyright © 2021 Danny Curry.

ISBN: 979-8224907427

Written by Danny Curry.

THE KILLER PREACHER :

THE TRUE STORY OF EDMUND LOPES AND OTHER TALES OF MURDER IN THE CHURCH

DANNY CURRY

"I'm the worst of the worst," tears streamed down the face of Edmund Lopes as he addressed his congregation. "If God can save me, imagine what he can do for you?"

To some, Edmund Lopes was a born liar and killer. To others, he was the epitome of a 'bad guy turned good' by the grace of God. But was isn't deniable is that he murdered two women and attempted to murder a third. He may even be responsible for the death of a fourth woman in a case that remains unsolved. Like many convicts, Lopes claimed to have discovered a Gideon Bible in prison and changed his ways. His manner and speech were so convincing that he eventually became pastor of a church in rural Washington. What his parishioners didn't know that their new pastor was more than just a sinner...he was a serial killer.

Edmund Lopes was born in Plymouth, Massachusetts in 1935. He had a seemingly normal childhood home with little in the way of abuse or poverty. His parents were Portuguese and he was raised Catholic. In his high school yearbook, his motto was "Speed is our safety over thin ice." He loved Louie L'Amour novels, country-western music, and playing dominoes.

He claimed that he joined the United States Marine Corps out of high school and played semi-professional football. But the slightly built Lopes stood only 5'3" and would be hard-pressed to play any position on the football field. He also claimed to be the cousin of singer Trini Lopez.

Tall tales aside, by the time he was thirty, Lopes life looked to be a mess. He had divorced his first wife and left behind four children. He lived with a woman named Helen Hanson for a spell. She would die of "acute alcoholism" at the age of thirty-four while living with Lopes. But ten years later police would want to question him about her death.

Because when Hanson died, a six-month-old baby was lying next to her. The baby had been left alone for four days before someone finally discovered her.

Lopes would refuse to speak about Hanson. He instead skipped town, leaving Massachusetts for Illinois.

"That was probably the beginning," forensic psychologist Paula Orange said. "Lopes was a very good actor. He could figure out what people wanted from him and give that persona to them. What he couldn't handle was his own 'demons', to use his Lopes' phraseology. He had something inside him that he couldn't control and it is safe to say that it manifested itself in his relationship with Helen and his later wife."

With very little in the way of job skills, he was hired to be the maintenance man at the Medinah Country Club in the suburbs of Chicago.

"I can't explain why I got into doing what I did," Lopes said. "I can say it was the devil. He makes things so fun, you know? It was the thrill of it all. I should have known what was happening to me but I didn't. I didn't have any guidance. I read about guys like John Dillinger. Al Capone. I loved Charles Bronson. Guys who just did what they wanted. I wanted that. I loved that. It was a thrill to, you know, do the things I did. I had nothing else going on, man. That's when the devil gets you. Idle hands."

A full-fledged criminal by the age of thirty-four, Lopes would use the alias "Jasper Lopes" as he sought handyman work around suburban Illinois. He would meet a forty-three-year-old waitress in a Bensenville, Illinois restaurant and eventually marry her. Phyllis Brown was her name and she mostly kept to herself.

But she stopped coming to work in June of 1970. A full month had elapsed before the police came calling to Jasper's home, wanting to know where his wife was.

Lopes was defensive, claiming that he didn't know where or when his wife left.

But he knew exactly where she was. He had killed her and buried her in a shallow grave of eighteen inches.

Days later, however, Lopes would be on the prowl again. Staking out local bars and golf courses. He would meet a woman named Shirley Johnson who made the dreadful mistake of taking "Jasper" to her home in Itasca, IL. They would live together for nearly a month before she had enough of his tall tales. She ordered him to leave but Lopes would have none of it.

He would stab and choke Shirley but she would miraculously survive the attack. Believing he had killed her, Lopes left the state of Illinois with the police hot on his trail.

"It was the adrenaline rush, man," Lopes recalled. "There was this compulsion inside me that I couldn't control. No matter how much I prayed it came out. I needed deliverance. But no one helped me. I couldn't help myself."

Five months later, a construction crew would find Phyllis Brown's body while they were installing a septic tank. Her body was badly decomposed and she was identifiable only because of the plaster on her arm. She had a cast placed on her limb some time before her fateful encounter with Lopes.

The authorities could not locate the dangerous Lopes. "Jasper" as he called himself, hitchhiked to Florida where he would be arrested for check forgery. He was then transferred back to Illinois where he would face charges for his wife's murder and the attempted murder of the woman in Itasca. It was an open and shut case as Edmund Lopes would be sentenced to 50-99 years for his crime.

But he would only serve twelve of them. In 1983, Lopes would be granted parole. He benefited from a law which only allowed parole board members to hear what the prisoner's plans were and their behavior inside the jail. They were kept ignorant of the prisoner's offenses.

Lopes rehearsed his parole hearing speech day and night before his appeal. Charming and affable, he knew the exact words that would tickle the parole board's ears.

So they released him under the condition that he did not leave the state.

Lopes didn't waste any time. He immediately left the state of Illinois, making his way into Nebraska.

Once there, he met up with a woman named Joan to whom he had correspondence with. Taking full advantage of their "pen pal" program, he regaled her with a story of his spiritual redemption. But he held no job higher than a maintenance man and needed a high-concept story of why he was in prison. So he impressed his future bride with tales of his time as a mafia hitman. This, of course, preceded his humble conversion to Christianity.

Joan had been in a bad marriage before. Her young daughter had been writing the convict initially before she took over. He sent her a photograph and they talked on the phone. Lopes let his "golden voice" do the work. Soon Joan was writing him every day.

On New Year's Eve of 1979, Lopes called Joan collect in Nebraska.

"Do you believe Jesus Christ is our high priest?" he asked. When Joan responded in the affirmative he asked her to declare their marriage vows over the phone call. "We don't need a preacher or a priest. God is our witness," he declared.

He nicknamed Joan as his "Angel." She called him "Lover Boy."

"What Joan experienced isn't exactly uncommon," Orange explained. "A lot of women become pen pals to prisoners. They're subconsciously attracted to the dark element of it all. She could construct whatever personality she wanted out of Edmund. He wrote that he had killed two women. That didn't bother her at all. He was a changed man. A Christian. The rationale was built in her from the get-go. She would put herself and her own family at risk by allowing this monster into her life. But she would see it that way."

Four years after exchanging their marital vows over prison phone, the two finally met.

On the run with his new bride, Lopes had picked the right state to escape to. Authorities in Illinois put Lopes on their "to find" list but seemed to have no sense of urgency in finding the violent parolee.

Two years later, Lopes and his bride would leave Nebraska, finding solace in West Richland, Washington. Lopes would reinvent himself, becoming a pastor at a small Baptist church.

"He was so convincing," a parishioner of the church whom we'll anonymously refer to as 'Wally' recalled. "You have to understand that these are people that are raised with the same values. The same narratives. So when someone comes along and repeats these same narratives they are pre-conditioned to accept them. Lopes instinctively knew this. He knew that all he had to do was tell them of his previous life as a sinner. In his case, he claimed to be a mafia hitman who killed over twenty people. And people in our church just ate it up. Because he was such a nice guy. He would go out of his way to help people. He would volunteer for everything. Visit relatives in the hospital. Be the referee at basketball games and the umpire for baseball. He was 'Pastor Ed'".

No longer "Jasper the Criminal", he reinvented himself as a Pastor. The small town of West Richland had less than 4,000 people. The First Baptist Church needed a new preacher. Only perhaps they didn't need another small-town boy who rose up from the ranks of the choir procession. Perhaps they needed someone who was born in the dark and saw the light. Or at least someone who acted that way.

The First Baptist Church of West Richland was just what you would expect. It sat in the basement of a cement block building. Lopes was given an "office", a mobile home that stood next door to the building.

"I tell you," Pastor Ed said to his growing congregation. "I have been to the bowels of hell. I have maimed and murdered. I was a hitman for the Mafia. The devil had a hold on me. But you know what? One night in prison, I just got on my knees and cried. I saw all of those

people I had killed flash before my eyes. Twenty-five? Twenty-six faces? I lost count. I asked God to forgive me."

"Chuck Colson heard about my story," Lopes told his parishioners. "He came down to see me. So did Billy Graham. I prayed with those men. I saw tears stream down their cheeks. They're just like you and me. They're sinners. If they can be saved. If I can be saved. Then God can certainly save you."

Lopes learned how to speak "Christian-ese". He learned how to manipulate language, manipulate the people in the pew to see him as someone whom God forgave. He played the role of the dutiful pastor. Visiting people when they were sick. Charming them all, young and old.

He would meet with a reporter named Wanda Briggs who wanted to write a feature about a "bad guy gone good." She was pointed in the direction of "Pastor Ed," hearing about the "golden-tongued" preacher who used to be a hitman for Murder Incorporated. Lopes was more than willing to give his story and Briggs began researching her piece.

During a sit-down interview with Briggs, he regaled her with stories of the anger he felt being a soldier in Korea, his fast cars, women, gambling and the weapons he used on his "professional hits." He told her about a sharpened stiletto that he strapped to the inside of his wrists and a 9mm pistol that he nicknamed "Betsy". He also told her that he stabbed his wife.

That was the only part of his story that was true.

When she started checking out his story, she contacted the authorities and found out that Pastor Ed was indeed a fugitive. He was sent to jail but his parishioners posted a $50,000 bond on his behalf, setting him free for the time being.

Lopes, of course, didn't waste any time trying to manipulate his flock once again.

He took to the pulpit the next Sunday, begging his parishioners for forgiveness.

The majority of them did.

But he would soon confess all of his sins.

"He fooled a lot of people in the church obviously," Wally recalled. "I remember another pastor came in after him from a neighboring church and saying something along the lines that we're the lucky ones. I don't know. It was eye-opening, that's for sure. For me, I learned that people need to hear certain things. Especially in church. If you give them what they want to hear then they'll forgive just about anything."

"Con artists have different victims," Orange said. "Sometimes it takes place in a pool hall. Sometimes in a used car lot. And a lot of times it happens in the church. Lopes was smart enough to know what to say to those people. He gave them the proper stimuli and they give him the response he knew he would get. It was rinse and repeat."

It was now 1992 and the now fifty-seven-year-old pastor had a slew of congregants who testified on his behalf. These parishioners would travel from Washington state to Illinois to give a good word for the man who in the words of one man, "led me to Jesus."

"You have to understand something," Lopes said. "I made up the story about being a hitman to get their respect. I had to show them how Jesus can transform a man's life. I couldn't tell them the whole truth. If I did that, they would judge me. But if I worked for the mafia they would respect that. And I didn't betray the parole board. They trusted me. I took the opportunity they gave me and became a new man."

The parole board decided to send Lopes to jail for an additional three months for the violation. Meanwhile, his congregation had wholly forgiven him despite the lies. They even built a new church which he would be pastoring.

Lopes would be released in May of 1992 and immediately headed back out to Washington. But Lopes wasn't true Pastor material. Only three years later, he would move to Missouri.

"The congregation soon grew tired of his lies," Wally said. "He would tell someone one thing about himself and tell someone else a completely different story. Some thought he was in his early sixties while he told some he was in his mid-fifties. He lied, even about little stuff. It was nutty. But damn, he was a nice guy."

Lopes prophecies that he couldn't "stay out of the Devil's clutches" would remain true. By 1997, he would be jailed again on a parole violation. The charge?

Bigamy.

Lopes loved women. He loved them so much that he married two of them. Shortly after he was paroled, he stayed with a woman in Westmont, Illinois. He had married her in 1980 but she had the marriage annulled in 1983. But this didn't occur before he had left Illinois for Nebraska to marry his pen pal.

"He had a golden tongue," his Westmont wife recalled. "Certainly I was fooled and I think the man used me to get out of prison. He pretended that he was a Christian. He is real good at that."

By 1997, he had been living alone and working as a day laborer before being arrested again.

He would be transferred to the Dixon Correctional Center in Illinois where he would remain until his death.

His "golden tongue" rhetoric could no longer save him once behind bars for this final time.

"I'm dying of heart and liver problems," Lopes wrote to the governor of Illinois. "I am no longer a threat to society and wish to be released to a halfway house. I work here as a hospice volunteer. While it is rewarding work, I do not want to wind up like my fellow inmates. Edmund desperately does not want to die in jail."

"His letters were a dead giveaway that he was a narcissist," Orange said. "He often referred to himself in the third person. That's sometimes a way for people to avoid responsibility for their actions."

To the end, Lopes didn't want to die in prison. He spent his days writing and re-writing a request for clemency.

These letters would never reach the desk of Governor Pat Quinn.

"He recognizes that all of the bad that has come to him in life was of his own doing," Lopes pleaded. "But now his time approaches, and he wants a few fleeting moments at freedom once again. Please help me."

No one would answer Lopes altar call this go around. He would die in prison and be cremated.

His ashes would be stored at a mortuary for over eighteen months after his death.

No one came forward to take possession of his ashes.

FATHER HANS SCHMIDT

For some people, the Catholic church has always been a place of respite. A place to practice their faith, and to commune with God. For others, the Catholic church has always been at the center of conspiracy and secrets. The Catholic church has always tried to keep the scandals that fall under their watchful eye under wraps, and for good reason. Many of them are so horrific that people would demand an overhaul of the entire system, for the safety of the victims. Of course, the scandals and conspiracies of the Catholic church date way, way back. For some, they are much more recent: in the last hundred years, or so.

Many people have different experiences with the Catholic church, that much is for sure. Despite the scandals, there can be no way to definitively say whether it's the church itself, or the bad apples that are drawn to it for the positions of power they can take up. For those who met with Hans B. Schmidt, a German Roman Catholic priest, their experience with the Catholic church would be their last.

With a Protestant father and a Catholic mother, Hans Schmidt was born in 1881, though the exact date isn't known. He was born in Aschaffenburg, a Bavarian village. He was born to a large family, and as a child, he was already religiously devout, nearly obsessed with faith. His mother had sewn him a child-sized cassock that he wore everywhere, often earning him the name of "the little chaplain". Not much is known about his childhood, but what is known is disturbing enough. In the early years of his life, Schmidt was known for having a fascination with the dismemberment of the body, as well as blood. As a child, Schmidt took to quenching this fascination with mutilating animals. His family members told stories of when Schmidt took the heads of his parent's geese and carried the heads around in his pockets.

It was also well known that Schmidt would spend much of his free time at the slaughterhouse. What better place to fill his need for dismemberment? He would watch the animals there be dismembered and dissected. Schmidt, in his later years, would admit that the sight of blood was what sparked some of his first sexual arousals. Through all of this, Schmidt had also taken a deep devotion to religious studies. He was devout, and though his otherwise strange fascinations lead people to be uncertain about how fit he was to go on to study Catholicism, he continued on to his seminary studies.

At 23, Schmidt claimed that he had been ordained by Bishop Kirstein, allowing him to finally serve as a Catholic priest. According to Schmidt, the bishop did so while they were alone, and that he would rather not speak of it at all. Schmidt also claimed that St. Elizabeth came to her himself in the middle of the night before he was ordained by Bishop Kirstein. He said that St. Elizabeth came to him and said, "I ordain you to the priesthood". Though, Schmidt also claimed he told no one, thinking that the others would make fun of him, claiming that he was also the butt of jokes for things like this.

Schmidt couldn't always keep out of trouble, though. His first run-in with the police was 1905, at the age of 24. He had been forging diplomas for students that were failing their studies. Despite a desire to see Schmidt punished by the public prosecutor, Schmidt evaded any charges due to the lawyer that his father had hired. The reason for the charges being dropped? Mental defect.

The mental defect might have been right. Schmidt was assigned to parishes in Burgel and Seelingstadt. While there, it was well known that Schmidt had unnatural tastes. He molested the altar boys under his charge and had affairs with the women in the church. It was even well known that Schmidt sought out prostitutes. As for his congregation, they didn't like him very much, either. Schmidt was eccentric. For a church that is so much about tradition and order, Schmidt's eccentricities didn't fit well for the Catholic priesthood.

After many complaints, Schmidt would not be assigned any more parishes. There was not much left for him to do but to find somewhere else to call home. In 1909, Hans Schmidt immigrated to the United

States, where he was assigned to the St. John's Roman Catholic Church in Louisville, Kentucky. Of course, that didn't last long. For the Catholic church, Schmidt was still eccentric and not well-liked in his new home. After some issues with the senior Pastor, Schmidt was finally transferred to the St. Boniface's Church, in New York City.

In 1912, while serving the St. Boniface's Church, Hans Schmidt met Anna Aumuller. She was a housekeeper for the Rectory of St. Boniface. She was new to the United States as well, having only been there for two years since emigrating in 1910 from the Austro-Hungarian Empire. Anna wasn't receptive to Schmidt's advances, at first. Still, Schmidt was insistent all the same. Schmidt had claimed to hear a voice of God that was commanding him to love Anna. Whether he really believed that, or whether it was a real mental defect, was unknown. In the end, Anna seemed to give in to Schmidt and the two entered a secret relationship together.

Of course, Schmidt's relationship with Anna was undoubtedly sexual. At the same time, beginning in December of 1912, Schmidt was also in a secret relationship with a dentist by the name of Ernest Muret. Not just his secret lover, Ernest Muret also ran a counterfeiting ring alongside Schmidt as his business partner. There was not much about Schmidt that seemed worthy of the priesthood. Schmidt's bisexual tendencies had been well-recorded in his youth. By Schmidt's own admission, he seemed to prefer his relationship with Ernest over Anna. Still, despite his desire for Ernest over Anna, Schmidt went ahead and married Anna in a secret ceremony.

The marriage occurred after Schmidt had been transferred to St. Joseph's Church in Manhattan. While he continued on his secret relationship with Anna, he also performed a ceremony to marry them - though, it wasn't legally binding. Still, he wrote their names on a marriage certificate and promised Anna that he would leave behind the priesthood to be with her. Perhaps all would have been well, had that been what happened.

It was clear through those who knew Hans Schmidt in his formative years that there was something not quite right about him. Even his lawyer had argued mental defect. Perhaps, this has been done at the time simply to get him off scot free. But, there was some truth to the claim. After all, most psychiatrists now look for the harming of animals as a child for the signs of a disturbed person. Back in the late 1800s, there was no such marker. While Schmidt had been an admittedly strange child, no one wound his fascination with the slaughter and dismemberment of animals to be anything other than that: strange.

One night, Schmidt was having relations with Anna on the High Altar at theSt. Joseph's Church. It was there that Schmidt heard the same voices that had told him to love Anna in the first place. Now, the voices were telling him something quite different. Schmidt claimed that a voice from God was telling him that he needed to sacrifice Anna at the altar, that God was telling him to do this. Of course, Anna told him that he was crazy and that he couldn't possibly. She didn't break it off with him, however. In fact, not long after the incident at the High Altar, Anna told Schmidt that she was pregnant with his child.

On September 2, 1913, Hans Schmidt committed a crime so heinous that not even the Catholic church could cover it up. In the night, Schmidt went to the apartment that he and Anna had rented under the guise of being a married couple. There, his lover slept, pregnant with his child. The voice of God had not left Schmidt, and they were still insistent about his need to sacrifice her. It was there that Schmidt slit Anna's throat while she was still sleeping. That might have been enough for him if there was not something clearly wrong with Hans Schmidt. After cutting her throat, Schmidt proceeded to have sex with her body while she bled out on their bed. He drank her blood as well. The whole ordeal ended with Schmidt following through with a life-long obsession: dismemberment.

Schmidt dismembered Anna's body and took it with him on a ferry, where he then threw it into the East River. After he had killed Anna and gotten rid of her body, Schmidt went right back to St. Joseph's Church as if nothing had ever happened. He offered the Holy mass and administered Communion, as though he hadn't just given in to his darkest urges.

On September 5th, 1913, a woman by the name of Mary Bann was walking near the docks along the New Jersey side of the Hudson River. She was walking with a male friend of hers, and it was there that she noticed a brown paper bade that was tied up with twine. It looked rather large, and Mary went to find out what it was. When she made her way down the side of the riverbank, Mary discovered that inside of the package was something no one should ever have to see: the dismembered piece of a torso, belonging to a young woman.

Not two days later, a man and his dog found the lower half of that very same torso. The body part was taken to the Hoboken Morgue, as was the upper part of the torso two days earlier. Slowly, the rest of the body began to wash up over the next few days, and the body parts trickled into the morgue. Two days after the second half of the torso washed up on the shore of the river, a fisherman caught something rather heavy on his hook. It couldn't have been a fish, but as he pulled it up her recognized it as something distinctly human. The fisherman couldn't pull it all the way up, as it slipped off his hook - but what remained was human hair. He thought, perhaps, that he had found a human head.

But by the time the harbor police arrived, they couldn't find anything. The body parts, though washed up in New Jersey, were found to have been wrapped up in newspapers from New York. The body parts painted a picture of a young woman who couldn't be much older than eighteen. She was obviously slight and small, maybe just shy over five feet or so, with dark hair. The autopsy of the torso also found the woman to have been pregnant, about five months along. On the shoulder blade of the torso was a birthmark, and that was how Inspector Faurot, who had taken over the case, got his first clue into who this mysterious victim was. Anne Hirt, a woman who worked at St. Boniface, came forward to police when she had not seen her friend, Anna Aumuller, in several days.

Anna Aumuller, too, had a birthmark on her shoulder and had confided in Anne about her pregnancy. Anne was able to identify the remains of Anna when she was brought to the morgue to look at the body. Anne was able to give Inspector Faurot all the information that he needed to begin the investigation into the murder of young Anna Aumuller. Anne Hirt had spoken to Anne about an "artist" that she was soon going to marry, as well as her apartment that she recently moved into, located at 68 Bradhurst Avenue

Due to the time that the crime took place in, 1913, there are two main accounts as to how Inspector Faurot found his way towards Hans Schmidt. In some accounts, it was Anne Hirt who identified young Anna Aumuller and lead him to the apartment and thus to Hans Schmidt. In other accounts, it was a stray pillowcase that pieces of the body had been wrapped in. In some accounts, the pillowcase still held a price tag to a manufacturer in Newark, which sold exclusively to a furniture store. In these accounts, Faurot found the receipts of a mattress, bed spring, pillow and pillowcases to an A. Van Dyke, and the delivery address to 68 Bradhurst Avenue. Whatever the account, Faurot was lead right to the place he needed to be.

Upon further inspection, Faurot found that the apartment was rented by a married couple and that the man who had rented the apartment went by the name H. Schmidt. Of course, it wouldn't have been long before Schmidt was found out. After all, he was no criminal mastermind. Still, Schmidt seemed to know enough not to come back to the apartment after he had disposed of Anna's body. Faurot stayed outside of Schmidt's rented apartment for three days, but no one came back. After the three days were up, they broke into the apartment.

The apartment was half-lived in, half-empty. There were all the signs that daily life had gone on in the apartment, from empty ginger ale bottles to a half dozen eggs. There were even pieces of infant's clothing, just waiting to be filled. However, there was something dark about the apartment as well: a terrible crime had taken place here, and Hans Schmidt had not been able to cover it up. Schmidt seemed to have made an attempt at cleaning. There was blood on the walls, having long dried. The floor looked to be recently cleaned, though poorly. Schmidt also left the knife he had used to slice Anna's neck in the kitchen, still covered in dried blood. There was a carpenter's saw, ostensibly used to have dismembered Anna's body. There were also pieces of bone still left in the bathroom. There were letters in the home addressed to Hans Schmidt, but there were also clothes left in the apartment that had the name A. Van Dyke sewn into the linings.

The letters gave Faurot more insight into who it was living in this apartment, and who he needed to be looking for. While some of the letters had been from women in Germany, others were from Anna Aumuller. The address on the letters seemed to come from 428 East Seventieth Street - though that was an old address that held no more clues to Schmidt's whereabouts than the apartment itself. Anna had left the 428 address after she had gotten her position at the St. Boniface's Church - where she had met Hans Schmidt.

The police followed Anna's life trail to St. Boniface's Church and were told by the senior pastor, Father John Braun, that Anna had transferred to St. Joseph's Church. When the police question Father Braun about Hans Schmidt, they were given their first real clue to both the body and the whereabouts of Schmidt. Father Braun told Faurot that Hans Schmidt had also worked at St. Boniface's Church, only to be transferred to St. Joseph's. This was all Inspector Faurot needed. He went to St. Joseph's Rectory and arrived in search for Schmidt. When he arrived, Faurot was met by the senior pastor, Father Daniel Quinn.

Father Quinn lead Faurot into the parlor, where Hans Schmidt stood in his clerical vestments: the handsome, dark-haired man of 32. He was otherwise a vision of piety. How could a man such as this, a holy man for all intents and purposes, have committed such a vicious and unholy crime? There are two accounts of what happened when confronted with the police, as well. In one account of Schmidt's arrest, he is asleep in the parlor and when awoken by the surrounding police, he tells them immediately that he was the one who killed Anna, stating that he had done so because he loved her.

In other accounts, Schmidt is not forthcoming. As the story goes, Schmidt at first denied ever even knowing Anna. However, Faurot and his investigators had evidence of the apartment in his name, after having already visited and found the lease signed by Hans Schmidt in the drawer. After being confronted with the lease, Schmidt then admitted to knowing Anna, but only wanting to help her in her time of need. After all, she was an immigrant just like him, working as a servant at a church. He told the police that he wanted to help her, and the only way he could think to do so was to let her live in an apartment he rented so that she could improve her station in life.

Unfortunately, the police had no other evidence that Schmidt was lying. Still, there was something not quite right about the whole thing. With a promise to return, the police had to leave to gather more evidence. In this account of Schmidt's arrest, the police found out through speaking with those who had known Schmidt over the years, that he had come to America under false pretenses. He had never been ordained, as he said he had all those years ago. The Bishop had never secretly ordained him, and he had in fact been suspended in 1907 by the Bishop of Mainz for falsifying documents to allow him to become the chaplain of a village called Buergel.

After gathering this information, Faurot and his investigators returned to St. Joseph's to speak with Hans Schmidt a second time. For a while, Schmidt tried to continue to say that his relationship with

Anna had been purely platonic, innocent if you will. He continued to insist that he knew nothing about her death and that he only wanted to help her improve her life. However, the longer that Faurot pressured him to talk, the more Schmidt began to admit. Finally, he opened up to the police and told them that he murdered her because his Patron Saint had spoken to him and told him to do it.

According to Schmidt, he had heard the voice of Saint Elizabeth of Hungary. She had spoken to him, a demanded a blood sacrifice. There was no one else who would do, and Schmidt knew that Anna was going to be the one that he had to sacrifice. Of course, Inspector Faurot wasn't so sure that Schmidt was telling the truth about the voices that he had heard. Though he didn't know that Schmidt had gotten off on mental defect once before, it was what he imagined Schmidt was setting himself up for again.

Schmidt then described the crime in all of its very last gory detail. He told the investigators how he drank Anna's blood and even called her slaughter a "butchery", describing it as "of a most revolting nature". He told Faurot everything about that night, and what he had done. He described dragging poor Anna's body, after slicing her throat and defiling her dying form, to the bathroom where he cut the body into seven different pieces. After he took the pieces wrapped in newspaper (or, by other accounts of the incident, wrapped in the pillow cases) to the ferry and threw them overboard, he returned to the apartment and tried to scrub away what he had done. However, the blood was stained on the mattress, so he took it away to a vacant lot and attempted to burn it, after enlisting the help of some neighborhood boys to make a bonfire.

It was around the early 1900s that trails of such sensation caused a wild media spectacle. After Hans Schmidt was taken into custody for his crimes, his story was no exception. The papers of New York City desperately competed against one another for the stories about Hans Schmidt. As for the trial, Schmidt was found to be an extremely competent manipulator. Whether or not the story of Schmidt having heard voices from his Patron Saint were true, he was able to put on such a show for the jury that no one could decide whether he was really insane or not.

Schmidt's defense was led by a man named W.M.K Olcott. Olcott was insistent that Schmidt had been consumed by his own delusions, as well as a "bloodlust", that meant he couldn't be responsible for what he had done. As a key witness, Olcott brought a man named Dr. Arnold Leo to the stand. Leo had treated both Hans Schmidt and Anna Aumuller months before her death. Leo was able to give some insight to the jury of Schmidt's strange mind. For example, Schmidt had at first claimed to be a music teacher when he met Leo, and it was only later that he told the truth about being a priest.

Leo described Schmidt as having been infatuated with Anna Aumuller, so much so that Schmidt had told the doctor that he was so in love that he was planning on giving up the priesthood. Leo also described times in which Schmidt would act erratically, often leaping up from his seat and playing an instrument before sitting down and speaking calmly, as if it had never happened. Still, Inspector Faurot was able to testify to Schmidt's scheming actions, in an attempt to prove that Hans Schmidt knew exactly what he was doing all along.

On December 30th, 1913, after the trail had been going on for 23 days, the Jury came back after 34 hours of deliberation. Unfortunately, there was no decision made. Luckily for Schmidt, his plan to plead insanity worked: the jury was hopelessly hung. The judge had no other choice but to declare a mistrial, and the whole process began again.

On January 19th, 1914, Hans Schmidt's second trial began. At the beginning of the second trial, Schmidt's lawyer insisted to the jury that he would prove that Hans Schmidt was not guilty by reason of insanity, the defense that Schmidt had been going for in his first trial. By some accounts, Schmidt made the fatal error of leaping up from his chair and shouting, "That is not true!" By other accounts, the Judge was the one who admonished the jury of the second trial and pleaded with them to make a decision where the first had not.

On February 5th, 1914, the jury took only two hours to come back with a verdict, convicting Hans Schmidt of first-degree murder. A week later, Schmidt received his sentencing: death. Of course, this killer priest con man was not about to go down without a fight. There was an incredibly lengthy appeals process which bought Hans Schmidt two more years while they dragged it out in court. However, no appeal was given, and Schmidt's death sentence was to be carried out.

By a jury of his peers, Schmidt was convicted of first-degree murder, the sentence for which was death by electric chair. He was sentenced to death on February 18th, 1916, three years after he had dismembered his "bride" for Saint Elizabeth of Hungary. As he awaited his death in the chair on the dawn of the 18th, he said his goodbyes and asking forgiveness for the things that he had done. It was there that he became the first and only Catholic priest that would be executed in the United States.

While Hans Schmidt was unique in that he was the first and only Catholic priest to be sentenced to death, his story is something that resonates with many cases throughout the years. For many predators, the Catholic church's privacy has been a way for them to hide their crimes, and to keep their victims silent. As well, for many predators, the plea of insanity has had jurors deliberating on what actions can be truly accounted for in the mind of someone who claims to not know what they're doing. In some ways, Hans Schmidt may be unique - but in many others, the world has known hundreds of Hans Schmidt's. The most we can do is learn from Hans Schmidt's story, and to see the patterns of these monsters who make sacred places their hunting grounds.

ARTHUR GARY BISHOP

Arthur Gary Bishop—also known as Roger Downs and Lynn Jones—was a child molester/serial killer who sexually abused and murdered five young boys near Salt Lake City, Utah, between 1979 and 1983; at the height of serial killing in the United States. His preferred method of murder was either drowning or beating his helpless victims with a hammer. He was ultimately executed on 9 June 1988 by lethal injection after voluntary waiving any appeal claims.

Early Life

Arthur Gary Bishop was born on 29 September 1952 in Hinckley, Utah, a very small desert town with fewer than 700 residents that lies 100 miles southwest of Salt Lake City in Millard County. The eldest of six brothers, Bishop was raised by his parents as a devout Mormon and excelled in school, earning honor roll status, as well as becoming an Eagle Scout. Despite defense attorneys describing Bishop as a "lonely, frightened child" during his trial, there was no evidence to support said claim. In actuality, he appeared to be a model son and devout Mormon and the specter of abuse never came into public discourse.

School classmates remembered Bishop as "a geek, rarely if ever finding someone who would accept the rare offer of a date." His election as business manager for the high school student council failed to improve his popularity and classmates, again, said that voting a nerd to student council was "a tradition" and "a joke to humble the social elite during the coming year."

Nevertheless, Bishop's younger brother Douglas, four years his junior, idolized his big brother. So much, in fact, that Douglas was arrested and convicted of molesting and sexually assaulting 26 boys between five and 17 years of age from 1976 to 1983 outside of Provo, Utah. He is currently serving four terms of five-years-to-life and, interestingly, the brothers were arrested within three days of each other; however, at the time Douglas did not know where his brother was or what he had done. Despite being diagnosed as a homosexual pedophile himself, Douglas maintained that neither Arthur nor Douglas suffered any sexual abuse as children.

Upon graduating from high school in 1969, Bishop served as a missionary for the Church of Jesus Christ of the Latter Day Saints in the Philippines when he was 19 years of age. Bishop then graduated from Steven-Henager College—a business school that guarantees its students with "fast-track, career specific education"—with honors with a major in accounting and appeared to be following a stable and devout path to success.

However, despite Bishop's seeming normalcy, he possessed a darker side that nobody could have ever guessed by his overt success. He was addicted to and enthralled by child pornography and cultivated and nurtured fantasies which elaborated upon the images with which he was so enamored. It is impossible to ascertain when Bishop crossed that line from his morbid daydreams into becoming an active pedophile; however, experts surmise that a year after his excommunication he finally succumbed to the evil within him.

In February 1978, Bishop was convicted of embezzling nearly $9,000 from a used car dealership where he had been employed as a bookkeeper and, based upon his alleged repentance whether genuine or not, received a five-year suspended sentence on his promise of restitution; however, instead of returning the money he, instead, disappeared. A warrant for his arrest was subsequently issued. His failure to surrender caused the Mormon Church to excommunicate him in October 1978. When Bishop disappeared, he ended all communication with his family and friends, moved to another city, and reemerged as Lynn E. Jones and, later, Roger W. Downs.

By October of that same year he took on the alias of Roger Downs in Salt Lake City proper. He joined the Big Brother program to spend time with disadvantaged youth and his charisma and pseudo-father persona attracted numerous children who he lured into spending time with him at his home or joining him on camping trips; thus potentially providing him victims. At one point, spokespeople for the Big Brother/ Big Sister organization admitted receiving tips that a Mr. Downs had molested at least two children while working with them; however, neither of the victims was Bishop's "little brother." Allegedly, police were notified but did nothing with the information.

The Crimes

Alonzo Daniels, 4

The first young boy to disappear was four-year-old Alonzo Daniels, reported missing on 14 October 1979 from his Salt Lake City apartment complex. His worried mother enlisted the help of relatives and friends to search their complex and neighborhood but the young boy was never found. When police started conducting door-to-door searches they first talked to neighbor Roger Downs as his apartment was across the hall from where Daniels and his mother lived. Bishop answered the police's routine questions and denied having any knowledge of the location of the boy. At this point, unbeknownst to the police and his mother the child was already dead.

Bishop had lured Daniels to his home with the promise of candy. He attempted to undress and fondle the young boy in his living room but when the child began to cry and threatened to tell his mother Bishop struck him with a hammer. This did not stop the boy's sobbing so Bishop carried him into the bathroom and drowned him in the tub. When the child was dead Bishop stuffed him into a large cardboard box and took it out to his car; walking right past Daniels' mother who was in the courtyard calling out her son's name.

Over the next few days hundreds of civilians and Salt Lake County's search and rescue team joined the hunt for young Daniels. Among the civilians were faculty and students from the University of Utah and members of a local Teamsters union. Descriptions of the child and descriptions of his clothing were printed and broadcast throughout the entire state. Police had questioned hundreds of people to no avail.

That night Bishop drove the corpse in the box to Cedar Fort, 20 miles southwest of Salt Lake City, and buried the child in the desert with only the trees that gave the nearby town its name as his gravestone.

While driving home, Bishop struggled with myriad emotions: revulsion at what he had done, fear of arrest, perverse excitement, and an overriding belief that he would, in fact, kill again unless he sought some type of help.

Kim Peterson, 11

During the year between Daniels' murder and his next one, Bishop pursued what he believed to be a less dangerous outlet for his uncontrollable and deadly urges. He began to kill puppies he adopted from Salt Lake City animal shelters. Such behavior is one aspect of the well-known triad of characteristics common to serial killers with the other two being bedwetting and setting fires. Over a span of 12 months Bishop adopted as many as 20 homeless puppies, essentially using them as surrogates for children. He later told investigators that "it was so stimulating" and that a puppy's whines were just like Daniels' own cries were. He would get frustrated at the puppies and then bludgeon them with hammers, drown them, or strangle them. It is unknown as to whether Bishop's neighbors knew of his activities; however, at the time, animal cruelty was a simple misdemeanor. Once he grew bored and discovered that the puppies failed to satisfy his urges Bishop went back to molesting children; using lures or threats to prevent them from reporting him.

The next young boy to vanish was 11-year-old Kim Peterson. On 8 November 1980, Peterson had spoken to a man about roller skates at the local skating rink with Kim mentioning that he wanted to sell his pair to purchase another. Bishop told the child he would pay him $35 for his skates. The next day, Peterson left home to go to the rink to sell them. Whereas both of Peterson's parents knew that he had found a buyer, neither of them knew who the mystery man was as no names were mentioned.

As Peterson had promised his parents he would come right home after the sale, when he failed to return they called the police and another fruitless search began. Witnesses at the rink reported that a child matching Peterson's description was talking to a white male, approximately 25 to 35 years of age who weighed around 200 pounds and had a full face, dark hair, and glasses, and clad in blue jeans and am army-style jacket was seen talking to Peterson earlier that day. One witness claimed that the man and the boy had driven away in a silver Chevy Camaro with out-of-state license plates; perhaps from Nevada. However, every lead was useless.

At this time, the police saw no similarity between their suspect and the Roger Downs who lived in an apartment a few blocks from the Petersons' home. Whereas they, again, questioned him routinely, they failed to make a connection between Peterson's disappearance and the disappearance of young Daniels the previous year.

Bishop had bludgeoned Peterson to death with a hammer and buried his body in the desert near where he had buried Daniels' body.

At this point, Bishop realized that murder was far easier the second time and surmised that there was plenty of room in the desert to bury children. While he still feared arrest, he spared his victims if they promised not to talk; however, he was discovering the incomparable rush that murder provided him that was better than any drug.

Danny Davis, 4

On 20 October 1981, four-year-old Danny Davis vanished at a busy supermarket in southern Salt Lake County while shopping with his grandmother. Prior to his kidnapping, Bishop (who later told detectives that while browsing through a local grocery store) "saw the most beautiful little boy kneeling in the aisle" as Davis was trying to get a gumball out of one of the store's machines. Bishop offered Davis some candy but the boy refused. As he was leaving the store Bishop happened to glance behind him to see Davis walking in his direction. He waited for the boy and then led him into the parking lot. Davis' grandmother couldn't find him when she had finished shopping and, as would be expected, panicked. Employees and customers searched the store and parking lot but couldn't find the young boy.

Witnesses said that they remembered a small boy near the gumball machine but could not identify photos of Davis. Others recalled a smiling man talking to Davis but could not give a clear description. They also reported that Davis was seen leaving the store with a man and a woman; however, the woman remains unknown. Witnesses also underwent hypnosis; however, while descriptions of the smiling man were clarified no identification could be made.

Police subsequently launched one of the biggest searches in Utah history trying to find the young boy. Fliers were printed with Davis' photo and copies were sent to law enforcement agencies across the country. A $20,000 reward was offered but nobody had any useful leads. Calls to the Federal Bureau of Investigation (FBI), the National Crime Information Center (NCIC), and Child Find were all to no avail.

Despite hundreds of searchers and the FBI scouring nearby neighborhoods, mountains, lakes, and woods, the young boy was never found. Concern increased as Davis was clad only in blue jeans, a t-shit, and thong sandals when last seen and the temperatures were dropping into the 30's at night. After no luck for two days, divers then searched Big Cottonwood Creek, ponds, roadside ditches, and even went through garbage dumpsters in hundreds of alleys.

At the time, Bishop—still under his alias of Downs—lived a mere half a block from the store and, again, was routinely questioned; however, the police still made no connection that the "same clueless neighbor" had lived in close proximity to all of the missing children. In fact, by the time police visited Bishop in his rented house, Davis was already dead.

Bishop molested the young boy and then silenced his crying by manually pinching his nose and covering his mouth until the child died. The following day Bishop, again, drove to Cedar Fort and buried his third victim beside the other two. Bishop believed that he had a foolproof plan as the Salt Lake City Police Department still had no clue.

After the fact—and much too late—neighbors did mention to police that Mr. Downs had an unusual fondness for children.

Bishop had no need for the reward offer as he still had ample money from his latest embezzlement scheme.

While Bishop was, indeed, cunning and was able to keep the police at bay, state legislators sprang into action as a result of numerous child disappearances. In August 1982, three-year-old Rachel Runyan was kidnapped from a school playground in Sunset; a mere 30 miles north of Salt Lake City. Discovery of her strangled corpse led to numerous calls for action by many organizations and the legislature passed another law.

Whereas first-degree murder was already a capital offense in Utah, the growing indignation with child abductions provided the impetus for the state legislature to add mandatory five-, ten-, or 15-year sentences for convicted child abductors. While this action was all fine and dandy it didn't get investigators any closer to finding out who was responsible for the recent missing children.

Eventually investigators dismissed any possible link between Runyan's murder and the missing Salt Lake City boys. However, there was still much speculation with respect to the disappearances of Daniels, Peterson, and Davis. Detectives from both the Salt Lake and Davis County Sheriff's Departments met with city police departments and FBI agents to try to come up with a lead. Since each of the boys had disappeared at different times of the day and on different days, speculation as to the abductor's employment was frustrated. Investigators also dismissed a clear link between the three boys as most killers tend to prey on members of their own race so while Peterson and Davis were Caucasian, Daniels was African-American. Additionally, Peterson was three times older than both Daniels and Davis. Thus any potential for a pedophile who stalked preschool children was dismissed as well.

By June 1983 almost two years had passed since the last child disappeared. That was to change.

Troy Ward, 6

Bishop's fourth victim was Troy Ward who was abducted on 23 June 1983, his sixth birthday. He was taken from a park near his home where he was permitted to play. Ward was supposed to meet a family friend at 4:00 p.m. at a predetermined street corner and the friend would drive him home to a surprise party. However, when 4:00 came and went with no signs of the child the friend drove to the Ward's residence hoping that the child was, perhaps, already there.

Police were immediately called and officers commenced searching the area around the park. One witness remembered seeing a boy who matched Ward's description leaving the scene with a man on foot just prior to 4:00 p.m. The witness assumed them to be father and son as they looked completely at ease with each other.

Of course, that man was Bishop who had just taken his fourth victim back to his home where—not unlike his other victims—Ward was sexually assaulted, bludgeoned with a hammer, and then drowned in the bathtub. Bishop later stated that he initially thought of letting the boy go; however, Ward's last-minute threats to expose Bishop led to his demise.

Afterward, instead of driving to his own private graveyard near Cedar Fort, Bishop drove east and buried the boy near Big Cottonwood Creek in the Twin Peaks Wilderness Area.

Bishop again realized how easy everything was and he decided not to wait another two years to kill again. He waited less than a month.

Graeme Cunningham, 13

On 14 July, 13-year-old Graeme Cunningham disappeared from his home two days before he was planning on attending a camping trip with a junior high classmate and their chaperone: 32-year-old Roger Downs. The boy was excited for his trip and was already all packed. That Thursday afternoon, two days before he was to leave, Cunningham vanished from his neighborhood without a trace; thus prompting his parents to call the police when he didn't come home for dinner.

The abduction made the news and Bishop visited Cunningham's mother to offer any help he could in finding her son. Police drew similarities to John Wayne Gacy who was convicted of murdering and burying under his house 33 victims and was seen talking with the last of his victims before that victim disappeared. The literature is rife with examples of serial killers who let down their guards and committed clumsy and costly mistakes. They wondered if Mr. Downs had committed a similar mistake by offering his help to his fifth victim's mother.

Investigation and Arrest

Bishop was again questioned. However, this time the police began to dig into his background and discovered his close proximity to all of the young male victims as well as an "almost unnatural fondness for neighborhood children." Sergeant Bruce White and Detective Steven Smith offered an invitation for Bishop to come to the police station to help find Cunningham. Veteran homicide detective Don Bell was waiting on their arrival and slowly and surely Bell began to pick apart Bishop's story.

They also discovered he was wanted under another alias, Lynn Jones, for embezzling $10,000 from an employer by writing bad checks in his boss' name before stealing his own personnel file from the office and vanishing. Police utilized the pending embezzlement charge to arrest Bishop to give them more time to investigate his possible link in the young boys' disappearances.

By sundown that day investigators had gotten Bishop to confess to five murders spanning four years.

The following morning Bishop took authorities to the Cedar Fort area where he pointed out the graves where Daniels', Peterson's, and Davis' remains were recovered. Bishop then led police another 65 miles south to Big Cottonwood Creek where Ward's and Cunningham's more recently deceased bodies were unearthed.

Autopsy results showed signs of sexual abuse on Ward's and Cunningham's remains. The other two had been buried far too long to provide any useful similar forensic evidence.

When Bishop's house was searched police discovered a .38 caliber gun, a bloodstained mallet and hammer, dozens of photographs of one of his victims taken after his abduction, and other pictures of nude boys which were framed to avoid their faces and, therefore, conceal their identities. Investigators also recovered a book entitled *100 Ways to Disappear and Live Free* that suggested that Bishop had studied how to be a fugitive from justice.

Additional investigation revealed that Bishop had molested dozens of other young boys over the years but did not kill them. After public announcement that Bishop was in custody and had confessed, the police were inundated with calls from parents who claimed that Bishop molested their children, or the children of acquaintances. His reasons for sparing their lives were never fully uncovered. Whereas a number of parents allegedly knew about Bishop's "activities" none of them had approached police during the four-year search for a child murderer, likely due to the fact that Bishop was a devout Mormon who tried to help disadvantaged children, or, perhaps, these parents did not want to admit or accept what happened to their children.

Bishop was charged with five counts of capital murder, five counts of kidnapping, two counts of forcible sexual assault, and one count of sexually abusing a minor; the sexual abuse evidence only applicable to his two most recent victims. Of course, murder was the charge that truly mattered in that if the state successfully proved its case Bishop would be sentenced to death.

Trial

Bishop's trial commenced on 27 February 1984 and lasted until 19 March.

Deputy County Attorney Robert Stott described Bishop as a "ruthless killer and sexual deviant possessed of 'a scheming, calculating, cunning mind.'" However, Bishop made his crimes sound awfully simple. He had said that one can offer children anything and they would go with complete strangers.

Bishop's defense team was led by Jo Carol Nesset-Sale who had very little realistic hope of getting their client acquitted as his confession alone had guaranteed that he would spend, at least, the rest of his life in prison. Therefore, his attorneys tried to mitigate Bishop's crimes in the hope of replacing first-degree murder charges with manslaughter. They argued that Bishop's emotional and psychological "deficits" drove him to kill and that "for some reason [he was] stuck or fixated with a sexual attraction to little boys. He never outgrew these erotic feelings. He was a lonely, frightened child." These words were later quoted by author Clifford L. Linedecker in his 1990 book *Serial Thrill Killers*.

His attorneys claimed that one of the primary culprits behind Bishop's fixation and deviance was pornography. Dr. Victor Cline was called as an expert witness and testified pornography had warped Bishop's mind to the extent that he was rendered unable to resist his attraction to children or to the murderous urges that followed. Bishop later stated in an interview with the *Salt Lake Tribune* that Dr. Cline's testimony made him realize what he was. He said:

"During my trial ... Dr. Victor Cline testified about the adverse effects of pornography. As I listened to his explanations, I could discern how my own life desires escalated. These normal feelings become desensitized, and they tend to act out what they have seen. So it was with me. I am a homosexual pedophile convicted of murder, and pornography was a determining factor in my downfall. Somehow I became sexually attracted to young boys, and I would fantasize about them naked...I would need pictures that were more explicit and shortly the images became commonplace and acceptable. Finding and procuring sexually arousing materials became an obsession. For me, seeing pornography was like lighting a fuse on a stick of dynamite. I became stimulated and had to gratify my urges and explode...If pornographic material would have been unavailable to me in my early stages, it is most probable that my sexual activities would not have escalated to the degree they did."

During his trial, the jurors listened to Bishop's taped confession that included admissions that he had molested his victims after their deaths. During the confession he giggled at times, mimicked the final words of some of his victims in a high falsetto voice, and also said that he was glad he was caught because he would have done it again.

Bishop also confessed that his offering help to Mrs. Cunningham was, in fact genuine. He wanted to allay her despair but did not know how to tell her that he had killed her son.

Ultimately, Bishop was convicted of five counts of murder, five counts of kidnapping, and one count of sexual abuse of a minor. Jude Jay Banks condemned Bishop from the bench and told him that state law gave Bishop the choice of execution by firing squad or lethal injection. Without hesitation he chose the latter.

Bishop later wrote a letter to explain his motives, reiterating much of what he said in his interview. He wrote:

"I am a homosexual pedophile convicted of murder, and pornography was a determining factor in my downfall. Somehow I became sexually attracted to young boys and I would fantasize about them naked. Certain

bookstores offered sex education, photographic, or art books which occasionally contained pictures of nude boys. I purchased such books and used them to enhance my masturbatory fantasies...Finding and procuring sexually arousing materials became an obsession. For me, seeing pornography was lighting a fuse on a stick of dynamite. I became stimulated and had to gratify my urges or explode. All boys became mere sexual objects. My conscience was desensitized and my sexual appetite entirely controlled my actions."

Soon after Bishop was sentenced, while on death row at the Utah State Prison at Point of the Mountain, there was a rumor that some unknown people had offered a $5,000 bounty for his murder, as well as another $5,000 for his brother Douglas' head. Prison Security Chief Captain Craig Rasmussen told reporters that these types of rumors occur pretty regularly but they had to take the threats against Bishop seriously because if he were to be attacked or otherwise injured after they had been given the warning then catastrophic results could ensue. There were no attempts on the lives of either of the Bishop brothers; however, their status as "short eyes" (child molesters) rendered them both outcasts within the prison hierarchy.

During this time Bishop was trying to rectify his Mormon beliefs with his current status. He said, "With great sadness and remorse, I realize that I allowed myself to be misled by Satan." This rediscovery of his religion led to a sort of repentance and some hope that he might actually survive, albeit in prison. His attorneys pursued a petition for a new trial but on 3 February 1988 the Utah Supreme Court rejected these efforts. At this time Bishop did, in fact, give up hope and resign himself to death.

On 29 February, Bishop filed a motion to dismiss his attorneys and to replace them with counsel who would be willing to abandon any further appeals. Following another competency hearing, the trial court determined that Bishop knew what he was doing and on 2 May the

Utah Supreme Court lifted his indefinite stay of execution and ordered the trial court to set an execution date.

Three days later, Bishop appeared in front of Judge Frank Noel—handcuffed and shackled—and read a brief handwritten statement that said:

"In reflecting back on my life, I remember a lot of good things, but these are overshadowed by the things I have done. I wish I could make restitution somehow, but I don't see how I can. I wish I could go back and change what happened, or that by giving my life these five innocent lives could be restored. Again, I say that I am truly sorry for all the anguish."

Judge Noel was unmoved by Bishop's words and signed his official death warrant, scheduling Bishop's execution for 10 June 1988.

Just prior to his execution, prison psychologist Al Carlisle told reporters that Bishop appeared to be a new man who had read the *Book of Mormon* ten times from cover-to-cover during his four years in prison and wore television headphones to drown out the profanity spewed at him by other inmates. Carlisle also stated that Bishop feared that his old impulses would return if he were ever freed. He added that Bishop demonstrated remorse during his entire time in prison and that Bishop believed that he would be entering the spirit world which will be more peaceful than on Earth. He also stated that Bishop didn't believe that he had been forgiven but he did believe that he could continue to work on his problems "on the other side."

Bishop then told prison officials and guards that he was "ready and anxious to die."

Bishop met with his parents for the final time on 8 June 1988 and then spent the remainder of his time alive by fasting and praying. Mormon Bishop Heber Geurts told *Salt Lake Tribune* reporter Robert Mims that it was unbelievable how calm and cool Bishop was during his final moments alive. Geurts added, "Even the guards can't understand it. I've dealt with thousands of inmates in 33 years, and he's the most sorrowful and repentant and remorseful man I've ever seen."

Whereas Bishop appeared to absolve his soul through his realignment with the Mormon Church and did, in fact, appear on all accounts to be extremely repentant, this neither eliminates nor minimizes the fact that he purposefully abducted five young boys, sexually assaulted them, and then murdered them; in addition to countless other children who he had sexually molested. These five boys are gone forever and their families are left to suffer their losses and Bishop's other victims had their innocence stolen from them; something they will never be able to recover. At least his own recognition of his deviant pedophiliac proclivities and push to stop any and all appeals in order to reach the death chamber as soon as possible did, in fact, serve to save an unknown number of other potential victims.

By 8:00 p.m. Wednesday, 8 June, Bishop had been transferred from his maximum security death row cell to a holding cell a mere 100 feet from the death chamber and, as is commonplace, was placed under 24-hour observation.

Twenty-seven hours later—just before midnight on Friday 10 June, Bishop was escorted into the 24-foot-by-24-foot execution chamber "with practiced precision." He was shackled yet did not resist, fully cooperating with the corrections officers. He was directed to climb onto the gurney that was bolted to the concrete floor in the northwest corner of the room and to stretch out his arms. Bishop did so without any hesitation. Utah Department of Corrections Deputy Director Bruce Egan stated that while Bishop was relaxed about the prospect of dying he was, in fact, "very nervous" about the execution itself.

Bishop forewent the "traditional" last statement to, first, dispel any rumors that he had been sexually molested as a child or had committed other murders and, second, to pray for his fellow man. Bishop said:

"By accepting my execution I do not consider myself a courageous hero or a noble martyr, or that I am giving up or that I'm going out in a blaze of glory, as some people have suggested. I am merely accepting my just

punishment as my conscience dictates I must. Though perhaps too little too late, I am doing the right thing now."

As well as:

"I leave this life with no ill feelings towards anyone, and I pray that the peace of God may rest upon each and every one of you. I know of God's love, patience and compassion, and have found comfort in that knowledge. When I kneel before Christ in the next life, having a perfect recollection of all my guilt, with a broken heart, I will humbly plead, 'Jesus, thou Son of God, have mercy on my soul.'"

Arthur Gary Bishop was ultimately executed smoothly and without flaw on Friday, 10 June 1988. At the time of his execution he expressed remorse for his actions.

By 12:15 a.m.—a mere nine minutes after his execution began—Bishop was pronounced dead by Dr. J. Brett Lazar, director of the Division of Community Health Services. Bishop's body was then taken to the state medical examiner's office for an autopsy before it was released to his family for the cremation Bishop requested.

Aftermath

Interestingly, the fact that Utah offers its condemned prisoners the choice of death by firing squad or lethal injection dates back to the early days of the Mormon Church in the 1850s when Brigham Young and Heber Kimball preached a doctrine of strict "blood atonement." This meant that sinners could demonstrate their repentance by spilling their own blood and if they failed to do so then other church members may be required to assist them. Thankfully, that grim doctrine is largely ignored today except by extremists such as Ervil LeBaron—dubbed the "Mormon Manson"—whose mass-murdering polygamist cult continues to practice it. Double killer Gary Gilmore chose the firing squad for his own execution in 1977 and continues to be the last to choose said method; however, the option remains on the books.

THE BRILLIANT SERIAL KILLER : THE TRUE STORY OF ISRAEL KEYES

MARK TOLBERT

Israel Keyes was an American serial killer who was active from approximately 2001 to his capture in 2012. He was known for his extreme attention to detail, his patience and discipline in selecting targets that lived far away from him. He was also meticulous in disposing of his victim's bodies as authorities have not uncovered any other evidence that Keyes did not provide.

Keyes killed several victims across the United States and was finally caught in 2012 after he uncharacteristically deviated from his modus operandi and hatched a plan to collect a ransom from his last victim's family.

Keyes was known to go to extreme lengths to hide his involvement in these murders, including driving across the country in rental cars, while using nothing but cash and removing the batteries from his cell phones in order to evade detection. This is uncharacteristic for a serial killer, since the vast majority of his contemporaries are known to have killed within their general geographic area.

While in federal custody in Anchorage, Alaska, Keyes would cooperate with investigators and admit to a host of crimes, including kidnapping, rape, and murder. Furthermore, Keyes admitted to committing a variety of burglaries and bank robberies to fund his killing sprees.

Early Life

Israel Keyes was born in Richmond, Utah in 1978. He was the second child to John Jeffrey Keyes and Heidi Hokansson. John, a maintenance man, and Heidi, a stay-at-home mom, raised their son in a Mormon environment and home-schooled both Israel and his eight siblings.Soon after his birth, Israel's parents moved the family to Aladdin Road, a small area north of Colville, Washington. While his family officially followed the Mormon faith, they were known to attend a local Christian Identity church, an organization rumored follow a white supremacist version of Christianity. Some, however, dispute this label and liken the religion to having parallels with the Amish church.

The family also quickly became friends with the neighbors, the Kehoe family. Chevie Kehoe, the eldest of eight sons, would later become an infamous white supremacist and convicted murderer, after killing William Frederick Mueller, along with his wife and daughter, during a robbery to secure guns, ammunition, and money.

During his time in Aladdin Road, Israel became a very introverted child with little interaction with the other children in town. He built his own cabin at the age of sixteen and preferred the wilderness over people. He is known to have burglarized several houses during his time in Aladdin, however, and is believed to have killed family pets for entertainment.

"When I was fourteen there was some friends staying with us," Keyes recalled. "And there was this cat of ours that was always getting into the trash. I had a lot of guns and I would always carry a gun and I shot it in the stomach. And it ran around and around the tree...and then it like crashed into the tree. I actually kind of laughed a little I think but..and then I looked over at everybody else and the kid who was with me, he was throwing up. Like he was, really, I don't know (chuckles) traumatized I guess you would say."

"Like most serial killers," forensic psychiatrist Paula Orange said. "Keyes built himself up to killing people by killing small animals first."

Following his family's relocation to Smyrna, Maine to become involved in the maple syrup business in the late 1990s, Keyes was kicked out of his family home for rejecting his parents' faith. His parents told his siblings to stay away from him.

"Keyes didn't think too much of his family," Orange said. "He was raised in a cult-like atmosphere and rejected the family religion, becoming very outspoken out his lack of belief in God. He had a Satanic pentagram branded on his back as well as an upside-down cross on his chest."

The rejection made Keyes want to tour the country and burn down as many churches as he could. Instead, he turned to murder and rape.

His first violent crime was committed sometime between 1996 and 1998, when Keyes abducted a teenage girl and raped her. Despite his later penchant for murder, he allowed this victim to go free. The identity of the teenage girl remains unknown.

Military Career

In 1998, Israel Keyes decided to enlist in the United States Army while living in New Jersey. Keyes served as a specialist in the 1st Battalion, 5th Infantry. He was subsequently stationed at Ft. Lewis, near Tacoma, Washington, and at Ft. Hood, near Killeen, Texas. He would later receive training in the Sinai region of Egypt.

While serving in the U.S. Army, Keyes was awarded the Army Achievement Medal for "meritorious service while assigned as a gunner and assistant gunner from the 2nd of December 1998 to the 8th of July, 2001 in the Alpha Company 60mm mortar section." Although Keyes received a DUI in Washington state in May 2001, he left the U.S. Army with an honorable discharge later that year.

Keyes would settle in Alaska and get a job working in construction. Incredibly, he would draw rave reviews from his employer who had no idea of the double life his new carpenter with the long hair led.

"Keyes was described as someone who was very professional," Orange said. "He had a tremendous focus and would work on projects for hours on end with intensity and focus. He would not stop for lunch. He would just work straight on through."

Keyes was described in a favorable manner by just about everyone else who met him. Words like "friendly", "low-key", "reliable" were among the adjectives used to describe him.

"The secret life was power to Israel Keyes," Orange said. "He got off on the fact that everyone he encountered had no idea who or what he really was. To them, he was a friendly carpenter who was on the quiet side. Mellow. But inside he was a raging killer. That is what gave him power."

Crimes

Bill & Lorraine Currier

After receiving his honorable discharge from the United States Army, and sometime between April and May 2011, Israel Keyes constructed a homemade silencer for his Ruger .22 pistol. Once he decided to kill, Keyes booked a flight from Washington state to Indiana. After arriving in Indiana, Keyes rented a car and drove the remaining 1,000 miles to the East Coast of the United States, using cash-only for the duration of the trip to avoid leaving behind any evidence.

Keyes arrived in New York to test his homemade silencer, then traveled to Vermont to pick up a murder "toolkit" that he had buried two years before. Keyes soon found an abandoned farmhouse in Essex, Vermont, which he identified as the location he would take his next victim to before killing them. He initially targeted random drivers passing through the rural area, intending to shoot out a tire on their car and kidnap them after they crashed, but decided to focus on a married couple after dismissing his original plan as unpractical and dangerous.

He soon identified Bill and Lorraine Currier, living at 8 Colbert Street, as his next victims on July 8, 2011.

Bill and Lorraine were 49 and 55 years old respectively. They had just celebrated their 25th wedding anniversary. Bill worked at the local university as a lab assistant while Lorraine worked at a nearby medical center.

"They were good people," Orange said. "They had a lot of pride in the upkeep of their Vermont home, manicuring the lawn and planting flowers. They were good employees and well-liked by co-workers. They were the epitome of upstanding, normal good people."

Keyes had picked the Currier's because they had no dog, no kids and a garage that would let him into the house. He stalked them for days, knowing their comings and going.

As one investigator would note, "Keyes was a serial killer with a system."

In the middle of the night, Keyes disabled the Currier's phone line and entered their house in what has been described as a "blitz attack." He ambushed the couple while they were sleeping and quickly subdued them, tying the couple up and stealing Lorraine's .38 snub-nose revolver in the process.

Once the couple was secured, he proceeded to transport them to the abandoned farmhouse in Essex. During the course of the night, both Lorraine and Bill attempted to escape the house. Lorraine was successfully captured and re-restrained. However, Keyes shot Bill with his silenced .22 caliber Ruger pistol in a fit of rage during his escape attempt. After killing Bill, Keyes sexually assaulted Lorraine and strangled her to death in the basement.

Following the killings, Keyes buried Bill and Lorraine's bodies in the basement of the Essex farmhouse, intending to return to the house at a later date to set fire to the building and thereby destroy any evidence in the blaze. Once the bodies were buried, Keyes set out to commit a robbery spree using the Currier's car.

"Keyes was spotted driving the Currier's car," Orange said. "The eyewitness quickly relayed this information to the police and they were able to come up with a sketch of Keyes. They were reported missing by this time and the authorities knew that foul play was involved. Things became particularly worrisome as the man in Currier's car was driving alone and the couple was nowhere to be found."

The Currier's car soon suffered "serious mechanical issues" and Keyes decided not to go through with his crime spree.

Keyes quickly abandoned the Currier's non working car in an apartment parking lot at 203 Pearl Street and proceeded to the White

National Monument Forest to burn the couple's belongings and to bury his toolkit and handgun.

Unbeknownst to Keyes, the farmhouse containing the Currier's bodies was bulldozed from October 25-27, 2011. The bodies, along with the rest of the farmhouse, were unknowingly disposed of at the local landfill.

The resting place lived up to Keyes' motto, 'Out of sight, out of mind.'

Samantha Koenig

On February 1, 2012, Keyes began to search for another random victim. He identified 18-year old barista Samantha Koenig, living and working in Anchorage, Alaska, as his next victim.

Samantha worked at a walk-up kiosk on a relatively busy highway. It was snowing that night, however, and folks were driving by too fast to pay attention to the man who walked up to the counter in a ski mask. This would not be unusual in Anchorage as the weather was freezing. Samantha greeted Israel with a smile and he handed her his travel mug, asking for some coffee. She would turn back around he had a gun pointed at her.

"Turn out the lights," he commanded.

Samantha complied.

"Turn around," he said.

Samantha began to cry, complying with his command. He forced her to empty the register then tied up her wrists with cable wire. After finding out that Koenig had a boyfriend who was set to show up soon, Keyes laid in wait for the boyfriend, Duane Tortolani. However, he quickly abandoned his plan to capture a second victim and dragged Koenig to his truck before transporting her to his property.

The next day, February 2nd, Keyes broke into Koenig's house. While there, he also burglarized her boyfriend's truck, taking the couple's joint debit card with him. However, both Koenig's father and Duane Tortolani witnessed this burglary and notified the authorities.

Keyes quickly tested the debit card to make sure that it worked and, upon confirming that it worked, he returned to his home and quickly killed Koenig, leaving her body in a storage shed located on his property. He immediately traveled to New Orleans, where he set out on a week-long cruise. However, once he disembarked from the cruise Keyes became increasingly concerned over the media coverage and intense police investigation of Keonig's disappearance and set out on a crime spree.

On February 16, Keyes burglarized and burned down a home in Aledo, Texas. Shortly thereafter, Keyes robbed the National Bank of Texas, attempting to kidnap yet another woman he saw walking a dog. Luckily, this potential victim was able to escape.

Other Victims

Israel Keyes is suspected of killing or attempting to kill several other victims. Keyes' first admitted violent crime took place sometime between 1996 and 1998, when he abducted and raped a teenage girl in Washington state. Unlike his later crimes, Keyes did not kill this victim. He released her soon after the sexual assault.

"My entire goal was to stay under the radar," Keyes said. "For a lot of this stuff, there wasn't anything. All I can say is that unless I talk about it, you're never going to find any evidence."

His first suspected murder is of an unknown couple in Washington State in 2001. Keyes also claimed to have killed another unidentified victim in Leah Bay, Washington in July 2001.

He planned out his killings like most people plan out their vacations. He would travel far away from his location.

From 2005 to 2006, Keyes is suspected of killing two separate victims. He confessed to these murders while being held at the Anchorage Correctional Complex, saying that these murders were committed on two separate occasions. Furthermore, he claimed to have dumped one of the bodies in Crescent Lake, located in Oregon.

"There is a history of this stuff that goes back a long time," Keyes said. "It's not something I've ever talked to anyone about."

Keyes just didn't rape his female victims. He would rape his male victims as well. It was something he was ashamed of as well as his necrophilia.

Following a multi-year break from killing, Keyes admitted to killing Debra J. Feldman in Hackensack, New Jersey on April 8, 2009. He also claimed to have killed another victim the following day somewhere in New York state.

Keyes would bury his murder weapons across numerous fields across the entire United States. Because of his military training, he knew how to maintain the weapons and return to them after they had been out of use for years. He buried these weapons in canisters filled with cable ties, ropes and drain cleaner.

During these trips, Keyes would admit to frequenting prostitutes.

Lastly, following the murder of Samantha Koenig and during his travels throughout the Southwestern United States, Keyes claims to have killed an unknown victim in Texas. The identity and final location of this victim remain unknown.

In addition to the actual murders that he committed, Keyes admitted to attempting to kill several other individuals over the years. For example, Keyes admitted to attempting to shoot both a couple and male police officer in Anchorage, Alaska sometime between April and May 2011. He also admitted to attempting to kidnap and kill a woman he spotted walking her dog in Texas, just days before his capture by a combination of Texas and federal law enforcement.

Other Crimes

Keyes was known to commit burglaries and bank robberies in order to fund his killing sprees. In addition, he admitted to killing small animals from the time he was a young child. He is said to have killed an unknown number of family dogs and cats throughout his travels.

<u>April 10, 2009</u>

Keyes robbed the Community Bank in Tupper Lake, NY in order to fund his killing spree. After holding up the bank teller with a .40 caliber Smith & Wesson (and with a .22 caliber 10/22 Ruger pistol in reserve), Keyes made off with over $10,000 in cash. Although he was filmed on camera during the robbery, his use of sunglasses, uncharacteristic clothing, and a fake mustache prevented him from being identified.

Following the successful robbery, Keyes buried a box with his robbery supplies in the Woodside Natural Area in Essex, Utah. He returned home four days later with the $10,000 in his possession.

<u>February 16, 2012</u>

While Keyes was traversing across the Southwestern United States following the successful ransom for Samantha Koenig, he committed two additional crimes. First, Keyes committed arson by setting fire to and burning down a 3,500 square foot house in Aledo, Texas. Secondly, Keyes again committed a bank robbery by holding up a teller at the National Bank of Texas in Azle, Texas, making off with an undisclosed amount of cash.

In all, Keyes is suspected of committing some 20 to 30 home invasions and burglaries during his lifetime. Furthermore, he killed an unknown amount of animals from his childhood to capture and is believed to have committed several unidentified bank robberies during his adult years in order to fund his killing trips across the country.

Capture

After murdering Samantha Koenig and leaving Alaska, Keyes concocted a plan to demand a $30,000 ransom for Koenig's return (at the time, police were unaware that Koenig had been killed). Keyes texted his demands and instructions to Duane Tortolani, Koenig's boyfriend.

At the same time, Keyes dug up the body of Samantha Koenig, dismembered it, and disposed of the body in Matanuska Lake.

The case became a high-profile one and community members chipped in to meet the ransom demand.

Thirty-thousand dollars, courtesy of a concerned and frightened community, would be deposited into Samantha's account.

After receiving the ransom money, Keyes began withdrawing cash from the associated account using her stolen debit card. There would be withdrawals in Alaska. Then Arizona. Then New Mexico.

The authorities would always be fifteen minutes behind the suspect when he made these withdrawals.

Israel would wear a "Scream" mask while the withdrawals but his 2012 Ford Focus that he was drawing was identified. The FBI noted all of their counterparts to be on the lookout for Keyes in this vehicle. It is important to note that Keyes actually exchanged his rented 2012 Ford Focus for another car to avoid detection; however, the rental company provided him with another 2012 Ford Focus for his exchange. This would eventually help to lead to his capture.

Police were then able to track account withdrawals as he traveled throughout the Southwestern United States, having made withdrawals from Koenig's account using her debit card in New Mexico, Arizona, and Texas. Interestingly, authorities had a video of Koenig's abduction but refused to release the footage to the public, a controversial move that many outsiders saw as hampering his capture.

Having left his sister's wedding just days before (where he became embroiled in a contentious argument about his pronounced atheism), Keyes was spotted speeding along Highway 59 by a Texas Highway Patrolman on March 13, 2012.

"The patrolman that made the traffic stop had no idea that Keyes was a wanted serial killer," Orange said "Keyes did not have his gun handy at the time. If he had, there's no doubt in my mind that he would have started shooting."

Keyes was placed under arrest by the patrolman and the Texas Rangers as well as the FBI was brought in. Authorities found the following items in Keyes' possession at the time of his capture: Koenig's ATM card and cell phone (with the battery removed), a ski-mask, handgun, and bundles of rubber-banded cash that was traced to the recent National Bank of Texas robbery.

The authorities still had hope that Samantha was still alive.

But Keyes would tell them nothing. He stared straight ahead without emotion as detectives hammered him with questions. Authorities would get very little out of him. He was thirty-four years old and lived a quiet life with his girlfriend and ten year old daughter in Anchorage. Everything about Keyes' past seemed normal. But he had a creepy withdrawn nature about his personality. When the FBI searched his property, they found out why.

He had searched numerous time on his computer for Samantha Koenig. The FBI would then confront Keyes with the surveillance footage they had of his truck pulling up in front of the kiosk.

"We know it was your truck," the FBI agent said.

Keyes would remain silent for about forty seconds before he finally spoke.

"Well, I might as well tell you everything. She's dead."

Keyes revealed that he had used a needle and thread to open up Samantha's eyes as she posed with the newspaper in the ransom photo.

Keyes would recount how he brought Samantha back to his home and tied her up. He had a glass of wine before he began verbally taunting Samantha by telling her what he was going to do to her. He then raped the victim and choked her to death.

Only twenty feet away, his live-in girlfriend and ten year old daughter were sleeping. They would wake up the following morning and he would join them at the breakfast table. Like turning a switch on-and-off, he spoke of taking his family on a cruise.

"It was apparent that neither his girlfriend or his daughter knew of his crimes," Orange said. "He would tell investigators that 'no one really knew him.'"

Shortly after Keyes' capture in Lufkin, he was then extradited to Alaska to stand trial for Koenig's murder. His trial was set for March 2013 and he was slated to be represented by federal defender Rich Curtner. Keyes was thirty-four years old at the time of his arrest.

Investigation

Israel Keyes was officially extradited to Alaska on March 26, 2012. Shortly after arriving at the Anchorage Correctional Complex, Keyes confessed to the murder of Samantha Koenig, providing information which allowed investigators to locate her dismembered body on April 1st of the same year.

Keyes was initially willing to cooperate with authorities and offered to confess and plead guilty to all charges leveled against him if two terms were met: his trial would last no longer than one year and he would be given the death penalty. He also conditioned his cooperation on the basis that his name and certain details not be released to the media and public.

"I'm not in this for the glory," Keyes told interrogators. "I'm not trying to be on TV. I want my kid to have a chance to grow up. She's in a safe place now, she's not going to see any of this. I want her to have a chance to grow up and not have this hanging over her head."

In June 2012, Keyes attempted to violently escape from a courthouse in Anchorage, in what authorities suspected was a spur-of-the-moment suicide attempt. Keyes was successfully subdued with a taser and taken back into custody alive. Following his attempted escape, Keyes was placed on a suicide watch, which entailed a prohibition on razor blades and sharp objects, regular inspections of his cell, and a 24/7 guard.

The next month, in July 2012, a local news station, WCAX, reported Keyes' connection to the kidnapping and murder of the Curriers. This lead to Keyes ending all cooperation with the authorities for the next two months.

Modus Operandi

While cooperating with authorities at the Anchorage Correctional Complex, Keyes described his approach to killing thusly: "I would let them come to me... You might not get exactly what you're looking for, there's not much to pick from, so to speak. But there's also no witnesses, there's nobody else around."

Location

Israel Keyes was very methodical in his approach to killing. Unlike most serial killers, Keyes did not kill victims who lived near him. Most serial killers conduct most of their kidnapping and abductions within the vicinity of their home, which leads to an easier investigation and higher chance of being captured. Keyes, on the other hand, was known to take cross-country trips in order to kill.

For example, Keyes killed the Curriers in Vermont while he was living in Washington state. Once he decided to kill, Keyes booked a flight from Washington to Indiana. He then rented a car, removed the battery from his cell phone, and paid for all of his expenses with cash as he drove 1,000 miles to the East Coast. He tested his homemade silencer in New York, retrieved a murder toolkit that he had hidden in Vermont two years earlier, and then identified the Curriers as his next victims. This type of careful planning, attention to detail, and restraint is very uncommon in serial killers.

Victim Profile

Unlike most serial killers, Keyes did not have a specific victim profile. For instance, Ted Bundy, another serial killer who shared many qualities with Keyes, was known to target young, white women between the ages of 15 and 25. However, Keyes had no such victim profile. He alternatively killed or attempted to kill married couples, young woman, men, and several other unknown victims. This allowed him to operate without substantial police scrutiny for some time.

Method of Killing

With the exception of his killing of Bill Currier, Keyes strangled every one of his victims. Furthermore, Bill Currier was shot to death while attempting to escape from the house that Keyes was keeping him and his wife at. Had Bill not been killed in the heat of passion while attempting to escape, it is likely that Keyes eventually would have strangled him to death as well.

Death

After accidentally being provided with razors while on suicide watch, Keyes committed suicide on December 2nd, 2012. He sliced his wrists vertically and hung himself while being held at the Anchorage Correctional Complex. He was pronounced dead immediately.

Prior to committing suicide, Keyes composed a four-page, handwritten letter that was found underneath his body. The letter was covered in blood and was largely illegible, but FBI forensic investigators were able to reconstruct much of his letter.

While the letter did not provide additional details about his crimes and victims, it did offer a glimpse into his psyche and reasons for committing murders. Keyes wrote "Family and friends will shed a few tears, pretend it's off to heaven you go. But the reality is you were just bones and meat, and with your brain died also your soul." Later in his letter he elaborated, "You may have been free, you loved living your lie, fate had its own scheme crushed like a bug, you still die." He repeatedly referred to his victims as a "pretty captive butterfly."

Dr. Stephen Montgomery, a forensic psychiatrist at Vanderbilt University Medical Center analyzed the letter and reached the following conclusion: "It has no remorse, no regard for human life or the victims and that fits with that type of psychopathic personality."

Authorities are still investigating various unsolved disappearances throughout the various states that Keyes visited. It is now believed that he may have targeted homeless shelters where he could kill people who would not be missed.

GWEN HENDRICKS

Gwen Gillespie Hendricks was born into a Navy family in Memphis, Tennessee in 1955.

Her father was a naval officer while her mother was a housewife. Like most military families, they moved often from station to station, according to her father's assignment. Growing up in a devoutly Catholic home and Gwen would embrace the religion with fervor.

Gwen dressed with modesty, wearing button down shirts and minimal make-up. She fostered a nerd look, with wire-rimmed glasses and short hair.

Carrying on the family's military tradition, she joined the Air Force at the age of twenty-five. It was there she would meet Jim Hendricks, twenty-four, who was her instructor.

Jim Hendricks was a tall, strapping Air Force sergeant with an air of authority. He had an easy smile and Gwen found him easy on the eyes.

"Well, it was kind of instant attraction," Gwen recalled. "There was a bit of lust there as he's a very tall, handsome man. The Air Force can tell you that you can't date but they can't tell you who to marry so I went to the Jag office and asked if I could marry my STA and they said 'yes.'"

The two were married in 1980. Jim had a five year old daughter, Season Hendricks, from a previous relationship. In 1982, they would have a son, Ben.

Because of their career choice, the couple spent a lot of time apart during the early years of their marriage. Jim was stationed at Wake Island while Gwen was assigned to Eglin Air Force Base in Florida.

The couple would be reunited in 1986 as Jim was assigned to the Air Force Academy in Colorado Springs. Gwen would not re-enlist in the Air Force, instead taking a job with the Internal Revenue Service.

The couple spent three years in Colorado before Jim would be transferred to Guam in August of 1989. He took the the entire family with him to the island.

"I figured we had a pretty normal family," Season said. "Until we moved to Guam. Things started to change. She (Gwen) would pick fights. She was jealous of the time my Dad and I would spend together."

"She (Gwen) had a different life in mind for herself," forensic psychologist Joyce Smith said. "She was used to having her own money. So when they moved to Guam there was little to do and less money to do it with."

Gwen and the children moved back to the United States, returning to Colorado and leaving Jim in Guam.

She would buy a home in Littleton and once again start working for the IRS. She then joined the junior Chamber of Commerce where she met Terry Knaack and a woman named Rochelle.

"Rochelle was into tarot cards," Gwen said. "And Terry was into new age occultism. My religion, my faith was still very meaningful to me. I wanted to do Bible study with them to get them out of what I considered witchcraft. Rochelle said she wouldn't go to Bible study with me unless I did the cards with her and the same with Terry. So I think I opened up the door to hell. Right after I started, everything went wrong"

During this time, Gwen began to experience health issues. She suffered from dizzy spells and nausea.

Her personality shifted as well, changing from being even-tempered to easily agitated and manic. With her health and ability to focus effected, Gwen stepped down from her revenue collector position to tax examiner.

"Could the illness have played a part in her deciding to kill her husband?" Smith asked. "Maybe. But Gwen was really steeped into religion and sounded like she embraced some of the more fringe elements of Christianity. She truly believed that occultism was a form of witchcraft and that those things could do her harm. So when she suffered from her illness she erroneously attributed it to her dabbling in the occult. She was a woman who preferred supernatural explanations to rational thought."

Gwen also started to grow deeper into debt, buying expensive gifts for friends.

In the fall of 1990, Gwen hired Terry Knaack to help remodel the Littleton home. A few months later, Knaack moved into the couple's basement with the rationale being he would be able to help with the mortgage. With the husband away and a man in the home, Gwen began to fantasize about Terry and starting over with him.

"Terry would talk a lot about wanting to having a ranch for children with special needs," Gwen recalled. "And I started having delusions that he and I would start this ranch together for the children."

"She entered into a fantasy world," Smith said. "She began imagining a life with this other man, having delusions of grandeur of what they would do together. He became her willing accomplice in her dreams, since her own husband was absent because of military duty. So an alternate universe with Terry Knaack became her obsession. What probably started as harmless day dreams soon grew into something sinister."

"I also believe that Gwen had more than a little bit of a Messiah complex. She had this compulsion to save people and it manifested in doling out gifts and handouts to people who she felt were in need. She had this secret life and kept things from Jim who was away on military assignment. Those secrets involved getting into credit card debt."

By January of 1991, Gwen began telling friends that she was having premonitions of Jim dying in a plane crash.

"I had this really bad dream over and over again," Gwen recalled. "Where Jim had died in a plane crash. I was thinking, well after Jim died that I would marry Terry and we'd start this ranch but of course Terry didn't know anything about because it was all in my head."

Gwen then began hearing voices.

"They (the voices) wanted me to sacrifice what was most dear in my life," Gwen recalled. "I remember thinking that I have to answer these voices because this is coming from God. You know, I've got to sacrifice what I loved the most and that was Jim."

Gwen kept a journal where she logged the "premonitions" of her husband's death. She titled the journal "The Courage to Will and Persevere," She described the voices that she heard and believed that God had told her to kill Jim.

"She experienced what we call 'command hallucinations,'" said Smith. "These are sometimes coupled with someone's value system, in this case, it was Gwen's religion. Gwen believed that she should obey God and believed that the voices that she heard were, in fact, coming from God. So this could go bad real quick if those voices told her to do damage to someone."

"She was past the breaking point, a delusional schizophrenic that was not diagnosed. When she confided with friends it was probably with people who shared her same point of view, people who believed in visions, messages from God and premonitions. Gwen was a soft-spoken woman and even if someone thought she was crazy they would not think she would be capable of taking a gun and blowing someone's brains out. She didn't have that violent vibe."

But behind closed doors, Gwen would deal with problems or difficulties in a haphazard fashion. She would often open up the Bible and believed that whatever random verse she came upon was a direct message from God.

"I reread Psalm 90 quite a few times before a small voice said, 'Keep reading, keep reading.'" Gwen wrote in her journal. "After reading the first page of stanzas, I knew I would be protected from the car bombs, the knifings, the guns, the contracts and all the other evil I had seen connected with busting the pornographers and pimps. Those mafia guys play rough, but somehow they just won't be able to get me. Then I turned the page to continue reading. It felt like a giant fist had slammed into my heart. I literally could not breath [sic]. I burst into sobs and sunk to the floor. I cried for Jim because he really was going to die."

Gwen began to prepare for Jim's death, taking out a $300,000 life insurance policy on her husband payable on his death.

She then visited a local banker, informing him that she would be soon be receiving proceeds from insurance claim. Gwen was told that she would not be able to use the money as long as Jim was alive. She then forged a doctor's note which alleged that she had multiple sclerosis. She submitted this note to the Red Cross along with a letter stating that they should be responsible for being her husband back from Guam.

Gwen did not want the proceeds from the insurance for her own material gain. She believed that she could use the proceeds from his life insurance to establish the "James Hendricks Foundation" to aid victims of mafia produced pornography.

"She became obsessed with pornographers," Smith said. "Like most people with Messiah Complexes, she chose an ill of society and focused on that, believing that she was a chosen vessel to help eradicate the 'sin'. In her deluded mind, she needed this money to accommodate God's will to establish this ranch wherein she would save victims of pornography. The only way she could attain this goal would be to kill Jim and take the life insurance proceeds."

"I was very desperate to have him (Jim) back," Gwen said. "I felt like I was at my limit and not really realizing that I actually was really having a breakdown."

With her husband not even dead yet, Gwen began purchasing clothes for herself and the children to wear for his funeral.

She bought silk flowers and boxes of Kleenex for mourning friends and family.

Gwen also increased the amount of Jim's life insurance from $300,000 to $1,000,000.

True to her premonition, she bought a wedding dress for herself and put a wedding ring on layaway for Knaack.

Gwen would ask God to speak to her directly and "guide her hand" as she thumbed through her Bible. When she got to a passage, she would believe that was what God wanted her to study."

"For the first reading, only the last sentence made sense," Gwen wrote. "I had asked if what I felt about Jim's death was real. He said yes.

God can even speak through the dictionary!

After reading the first page of stanzas, I knew I would be protected from car bombs, the knifings, the guns, the contracts and all the other evil I had seen connected with busting pornographers and pimps. Those Mafia guys play rough, but somehow they just won't be able to get me."

"You can see her delusions of grandeur in her journal writings," Smith said. "She had all of the symptoms of a delusional narcissist, truly believing that God made her as the 'Chosen One.'"

Gwen would write that she had a two-way conversation with God about creating the ranch.

"Oh, so the ranch is in Douglas county near to the Springs so my family will be protected from the mafia guys' Then I knew in Denver, I'm Gwen Hendricks. In the Springs, I'm Gwen Knaack. I had thought the clinic would carry the name of the ranch, but with this new insight, I knew that for safety sake, everything had to be kept separate."

She continued to have health issues as well, as the nausea and attacks of dizziness still had not subsided. Physicians could not determine the cause of her illness. She was eventually diagnosed with Ménière's disease, an ailment that causes vertigo and a fluctuating hearing loss. She had a micro-shunt placed into her ear which only helped relieve the pain she was experiencing.

Her mental health, however, continued to deteriorate.

Jim would return to Colorado for good in May of 1991. It would not be a well-received reunion, however, as the couple fought over everything specifically the living arrangements of Knaack. Jim promptly kicked the boarder out of the home.

He then took control of the finances as he discovered that Gwen had maxed out the credit cards.

"My brother said that she had apparently taken several other credit cards and had maxed them out to the limit," recalled Steve Hendricks, Jim's brother. "And he was furious with her at that point. He did confide in me that he was thinking about leaving Gwen."

Jim would take away all of Gwen's credit cards and this made her extremely angry.

"He took away her power," Smith said. "She got an ego boost by buying expensive gifts for friends and helping out women that she thought were in need. When Jim took that away, she saw him as someone who needed to be eliminated."

Divorce seemed imminent but Gwen seemed immune to it all in her journal writings.

"The funeral, the ranch school, children, the foundation, always being pushed forward," she wrote. "I have to do what I have to do, too. But just for now I'm going to take one day at a time. I'm hoping I don't get too compulsed to do anything more for at least this coming week. I need to rest.

Perhaps I should start by explaining the little voice. It's my voice, but not me. It comes from somewhere inside, and if I don't listen to it, act on it, it becomes a compulsion. If I don't listen and act on the compulsion, it grows stronger and stronger until it dominates all aspects of my life. I learned long ago to listen and do what I'm told. Things work out when I do, and when I don't, things get real miserable...Yes, my little voice is the way God reaches me with the Holy Spirit."

With Jim now home on a permanent basis, The voices in her head grew louder. They began to speak with more urgency in telling her that she had to kill her husband.

"True to her religious background, she did not interpret auditory hallucinations as a sign of mental illness," Smith said. "Gwen was the kind of woman who took the stories in the Bible literally, seeing herself as a modern day Abraham who heard voices from God. You hear it in the way she describes the voices in her head telling her to sacrifice her husband in the same way the Bible speaks of God telling Abraham to sacrifice his son Isaac."

"I said 'Lord I surrender to you,'" Gwen recalled. "I'm hearing voices from God and this is what God wants and I have to get this from God and if this is what God wants then I have to give it to him. So I went out and I bought a gun"

"The voices in her head told her it was time," Smith said. "And true to her value system, she had to obey. For her religion was not a therapeutic aid because of the way she had viewed it. Her God was a vengeful one, a violent one."

On Friday, August 17th, 1991 Gwen drove to Peterson Air Force Base to meet with her husband, a 75 mile drive, to bring him a change of clothes.

"Jim was working late and he asked me to bring him something to eat." Gwen said.

She had informed police that Jim was working all night to prepare for an inspection but changed his mind.

Gwen wrote in her journal about the incident.

When Jim called to say he was on his way home, I went into shock. I knew the time was at hand. I knew I wasn't really ready. I screamed and cried and raged. Then I asked again, if he was meant to die or was I just suckered into some kind of head game. Benjamin's daddy died. I cried myself to sleep that night. I thought what was I supposed to do with two husbands. God has the oddest sense of humor."

"She told me that she was gonna make a nice little picnic for them," Gwen's step-daughter Season recalled. "They were going to make a night of it and that she wanted him to feel good for his inspection."

Gwen left the home and dropped off both Season and son Ben with a friend. When Gwen arrived at the Air Force base, however, she stated that Jim told her that he was heading home. She maintained that the two then went back home in separate cars.

"His truck was in the lead," Gwen said. "I was in the car behind. I remember being so tired, I told him I can't go on anymore. I just want a quick nap and let's get in the back of the truck."

She said that they traveled in separate cars but she became tired and slept through the night at a rest stop along Interstate 25.

Police, however, believed that Gwen lured Jim to an abandoned stretch of highway with the promise of sex.

The two met at the side of the road and Gwen hesitated when thinking of pulling out the gun. She wanted her husband to go peacefully.

"I took the gun out from underneath the seat of the car," Gwen said. "I got into the truck and laid next to him and when I could feel that he was deeply sleeping that's when I shot him."

Gwen would shoot Jim six times.

"It was like I was outside of myself," Gwen said. "Looking and watching what I was doing. I felt very numb, very cold, like I was on auto-pilot. I got back into my car and I took apart the gun and I was just throwing the parts out the window and just driving around, just in a fog, not knowing what I was doing, where I was going. I stopped at a roadside rest stop. Fell asleep. When I woke up and I didn't know everything that happened."

When Gwen arrived back home that Saturday she began making calls to the police, stating that her husband was missing.

On Monday morning, she called Jim's supervisor who sent out two officers to search for him.

One of his co-workers would find his pickup truck on the side of Highway 83 in Douglas County. His body had been placed in the camper shell in back of his truck.

He had been shot six times in the chest and neck with a small caliber handgun.

Gwen would become the primary suspect.

Police noted that she hardly showed any emotion when they informed her of her husband's death.

"Her state of mind was that of a wife with a missing husband," one of the deputies recalled. "When she was telling a story, she couldn't stick with the same story. And that's a clue, obviously, to law enforcement."

Gwen would then break the news to Jim's daughter, Season.

"Gwen said they found him by the side of the road in his car," Season said. "And that he had been murdered. I don't remember her crying. It was the worst moment of my life."

Terry Knaack would be helpful in the case against Gwen. She had been secretly in love with him and given him her diary. He read through her writings and promptly delivered the diary to the Douglas County Sheriff's Department. The sheriffs then instructed him to call Gwen while they would listen in.

Gwen would tell Knaack that she didn't kill Jim but that she wanted to die. Then Douglas County Sheriff's Department Kim Castellano's intuition told her something was wrong. The Hendricks had two pre-teens, a boy and a girl and the boy was never around during questioning.

Castellano believed that Gwen had a problem with males. With one of the male investigators, an Air Force official, by her side, Castellano went back to talk to Gwen.

Once again, the boy was not there. Gwen was overly polite to Castellano, asking her if she wanted anything to eat and jumping up to fix her something before she could answer.

Gwen would totally ignored the male detective.

Castellano used this knowledge to her advantage and befriended Gwen, sensing that the delusional woman would be much more forthcoming with a female officer than a male.

Gwen began trusting her enough that she asked for Castellano's help in balancing her check book. The detective then saw that Hendricks had recently taken out several insurance policies that would be hers when her husband died.

The investigators then used a technique police refer to as the "midnight confession." Castellano and the Air Force official went over to the Hendricks house at eleven at night, waking Gwen up.

Questioning her in the family room, Gwen continued to deny her involvement in her husband's killing. Castellano and her partner then took turns reading from Gwen's journal, tightening the screws on her denial. They also saw Jim's watch on the counter.

Castellano then told her to get dressed and that she was being taken in.

Gwen finally cracked. She curled into a fetal position and confessed.

"Two stories that night—the story of the rest area and the story of Highway 83," she sobbed.

Gwen would go on to describe the highway story.

"There is blood everywhere, I can see it everywhere," she said. "It's terrible. My mind won't let me remember. I don't know if I shot him or not. I don't know what's real anymore."

Gwen was then taken to a local hospital where she stayed for two days for a mental health evaluation. She was arrested upon release and charged with her husband's murder.

After undergoing another mental health examination, Gwen was deemed delusional but understood the charges being levied against her.

Because of this, she was found fit to stand trial.

In court, however, Gwen continued to state that she didn't kill her husband. She said that the body found at the crime scene was not Jim's.

"There was the obvious choice for her attorneys to declare her insane," Smith said. "She had one hell of an imagination and could make things up on the fly. She said during the trial that she became completely convinced that her husband was still alive, going into full blown denial. 'He's still alive, he's out there somewhere and you have to find him', she would say. She was completely delusional."

Her first attorney, Lloyd Boyer, stated that it was physically impossible for Gwen to have murdered Jim Hendricks.

"The lack of gunshot residue inside the Capitol (Jim's car) vehicle," Boyer said. "Indicated that the murder had not occurred in the vehicle. Mr. Hendricks was quite a bit larger than Gwen and she was small, not especially strong and could not have moved the victim into the vehicle."

The investigators failed to produce the gun that Gwen used but the prosecution had another tool at its disposal.

The first link was Jim's watch that they found in Gwen's possession, which showed that she had tampered with the crime scene. The prosecution showed how she was going to use the money from the insurance policies and start a "home for troubled people" that would be near the spot where she killed her husband.

The jury found her guilty of first-degree murder and Hendricks was sentenced to life in prison.

"I just kept my faith that Jim would come rescue me and I would be set free from prison," Gwen said. "Of course, that never happened."

Inside the prison, physicians deemed her to be mentally unfit to be included with the general population and transferred her to the psychiatric unit.

"They got me on anti-psychotics," Gwen said. "And anti-depressants but it wasn't until 1997 that I started having memories of what had happened. At first, it was like just pictures and they hit me like bricks, you know. I killed a great husband and Dad. I robbed Season and Ben of their father. I felt lower than dirt."

She did have help, however, as some legal advocates filed briefs on her behalf, claiming that she had been insane at the time of her trial.

In September of 2000, the Supreme Court of Colorado overturned Gwen's conviction and ordered a new trial.

In April of 2001, a judge ruled that Gwen was not guilty by reason of insanity.

The trial lasted ten minutes.

"She came to terms with what she had done," Smith said. "She had stopped protesting, stop denying and admitted to what she had done."

Gwen was then remanded to a psychiatric care facility in Colorado. She then decided to change her name to "Emi Masai".

"When I lost Jim," Gwen said. "I also lost my children. I longed to be a wife and mother again. I redefined myself as married to Christ and being a mother to all the people I meet."

"By renaming herself she thought that she could obtain a new identity," Smith said. "It was a way of divorcing herself from her past transgressions."

Gwen went through four years of psychiatric treatment where the physicians determined that she was no longer a threat to society. She was released to a residential program where she now helps the needy at Mercy Ministries.

She continues to take her anti-psychotic medication.

"I never want to slip back into mental illness again," Gwen said. "I literally thank God every morning I open my medicine cabinet. I've always said justice wasn't done. Justice in this case would have been my execution. A life for a life. But it's not about fairness. It's about recognizing mental illness and knowing that you're not responsible for what you are doing when you're psychotic."

Gwen has had minimal contact with both her son and step-daughter since she committed the murder of their father.

"I long to see them but they let it be known through family channels that they don't want to see me," Gwen said. "So I respect that."

"I'm really glad that Gwen has helped herself enough to admit what she's done," Season said. "And I hope there never is a time where it gets easy for her to look in the mirror. Because there's never a time where it's easy to be without our Dad."

"I wish I could take it back," Gwen said. "Be a good wife and Mom again. I can't turn the clock back. So all I can do is give them my deepest apology and ask them to forgive me."

FATHER JOHN FEIT

ANA BENSON

The Catholic Church is known for sweeping everything under the rug and keeping their secrets from coming out. In the 1990s, the public finally found out about the sexual abuse that was predominant in this religious institution. Having in mind that they managed to cover up numerous cases throughout the decades, it shouldn't come as a surprise that they also concealed a murder which shocked a small town of McAllen in 1960.

Religious people from this area refused to believe that a priest was capable of such a thing, and the police had almost no evidence. The case went cold, and it collected dust for decades, waiting for someone to start talking. And luckily, one person decided to tell the investigators everything.

Early life

John Feit was born in Chicago, Illinois in 1933. He was a quiet and shy boy, who always kept to himself. John was a good student, and his parents never had any issues with him during his adolescence. The family was highly religious, so they weren't surprised when John informed them that he was planning to become a priest. His parents supported this decision, and soon enough, John Feit started his training. But one of his friends would later say that when they asked John why he became a priest, he answered: *"I just wanted to give it a try."*

Father John Feit's life as a priest was a busy one. He was constantly traveling, which was not a problem for him. However, the Catholic Church sent the young man to Texas at the end of the 1950s, where he remained for years. His parishioners liked him, and they often described Father John as very sympathetic and eager to help.

The disappearance of Irene Garza

McAllen is a town located in Hidalgo County which is often called Rio Grande Valley. Since it is near the border between Texas and Mexico,

McAllen has a strong Latino community. The Garza family immigrated to the United States, and they started a dry cleaning business. The success was immediate, and they relocated to the northern part of McAllen after just a couple of years. It housed wealthier and more prominent citizens. The Garza family was religious, and the members rarely missed the opportunity to visit their local church on a daily basis.

Irene Garza was the pride and joy of her parents. She attended McAllen High School and became a head drum majorette. Irene even competed in Miss All-South Texas Sweetheart in 1958 and won the title that year. Determined to continue her education, Irene Garza enrolled in Pan American College where she studied to become a teacher. After getting her diploma, Irene Garza moved back to McAllen, Texas. She wanted to help her community and work with kids from marginalized families. She taught lower grades in an elementary school and was selected to be a secretary of the PTA.

But no matter how busy she was, Irene Garza would always show up for a mass at the Sacred Heart Church. It was Saturday, April 16th, 1960 when Irene took her family's car in order to attend the evening confession. She left the driveway at 06:30 PM, ensuring her mother that she will be back soon. Irene Garza did arrive at the church, and she was seen by several parishioners who were there at the same time. The church was crowded because it was Easter. One of them remembered that Irene asked him politely if she could step in front of him in the line for the confession because she was in a hurry. However, nobody can confirm that they saw Irene exit the church. She never came home that night, but her family wasn't too worried. The midnight mass was scheduled for the night, so they thought she stayed there. However, the parents didn't hear from Irene in the morning. They went straight to the church, but the only thing they found was Garza's family car parked in the street. There was no sign of Irene.

The police were informed about the disappearance, and soon enough the whole town of McAllen knew that the beloved schoolteacher was missing. Everyone was on a lookout, hoping that they would spot Irene somewhere. But the discovery of the first clue suggested that something sinister might have happened to this young woman. P.W.Miller was walking down McColl Road when he noticed a high-heeled left shoe near a curb. This happened two days after the disappearance. The road itself was pretty out of the way, so it is not surprising that no one noticed it sooner. The police officers picked it up as an evidence and presented the shoe to Irene's parents. They confirmed that the shoe belonged to their daughter.

Only one day later, Alfredo Barrera who was also a teacher saw something suspicious in a field which was fairly close to McColl Road. He decided to investigate and discovered a black female purse. Knowing that Irene Garza was missing, he picked it up with a stick in order not to destroy any possible traces. The detectives analyzed the evidence, but they couldn't find any fingerprints on the purse. They did find Irene's driving license in one of the inside pockets. This second discovery was very important because it gave the investigators a clue about the direction Irene's kidnapper or the possible killer was taking. They went further up north and found a piece of white lace. The detectives recalled that a couple of parishioners mentioned that Irene was wearing it on her head when she went for a confession.

The search and the leads

Hidalgo County Sheriff's Office was certain that it was time for a full search of the area. They gathered up seventy officers who started combing through the surrounding fields, groves, and woods in hopes of finding more traces of Irene. Other police officers focused on Sacred Heart Church, making it the center of the search. They knocked on every door and asked anyone if they saw Irene on the night of the disappearance. The search widened in the following days, and divers were searching the canals. Border Patrol offered two of their planes, and National Guardsmen were on the ground as well. It was the biggest search for a missing person in southern Texas.

The newspapers all around the state printed stories about Irene Garza, and this generated plenty of tips. The detectives checked out every lead, and they even went to question a tourist in Edinburg, which is a small town close to McAllen. The man threatened a waitress working at the Highway Grill, and he told her that he killed Irene Garza. He changed his story as soon as the authorities arrived, defending himself by saying that he was on a vacation and couldn't handle his alcohol well. Another promising lead was a call from Irene herself. A woman phoned the Garza residence saying that she was kidnapped and locked in a hotel room. She gave an address in Hidalgo. The police rushed there immediately, but it was just a prank.

The discovery of the body

Five days after the disappearance, McAllen Police Department got a call. They were informed that a passerby saw a body of a woman in the Second Street canal. The detectives were there immediately, struggling to get through the crowd that was gathering on the banks. And sure enough, a body was floating in the water. Once they pulled Irene up to the shore, the initial examination showed that she was dressed in her clothes, but the shoes and the underwear were missing. There were some wounds on her face, including two black eyes.

Irene's body was transported to the examiner who determined the cause of death. Irene Garza died of suffocation, but she was also beaten prior to her death, possibly with a blunt object. The detectives who pulled her body from the canal suspected that she was sexually assaulted as well. The coroner confirmed this, adding one disturbing fact: Irene was raped while being in a coma from the blunt force trauma to her head. Irene's parents were unable to go to the morgue in order to identify the body. The whole situation was very emotional to them, so the brother-in-law offered to go instead. Once the man viewed the body, he broke down, leaving the room as soon as possible. However, he did confirm that the body found in the Second Street canal was, in fact, Irene Garcia.

The whole town of McAllen was in shock after the details of the murder got published in the local newspapers. The fear was growing because nobody knew if there was a serial killer hiding among them, or if this was a work of a transient person simply passing through. A magazine from Monterrey, Mexico sparked a debate among the residents of McAllen because they suspected that the killer was Leo de Leon. De Leon died a couple of days after the murder, suffering a fatal heart attack. However, the most interesting rumor was that a priest from the Sacred Heart Church murdered Irene Garza.

The initial investigation

Irene Garza was found in a body of water so collecting any physical evidence from her body was near impossible. If there was any DNA, it was washed away. It was difficult to find a person of interest when the detectives had absolutely no leads. All of those interviews conducted during the search for Irene didn't provide any clues, and it seemed like nobody saw anything suspicious on that Saturday night when Irene vanished into thin air. Hoping they could find something on the shore, the investigators took a closer look at the banks of the canal. Sheriff's Deputy noticed a muddy shoe print and one thing stood out to him right away – there was a single hair from Irene's head in the mud underneath.

Irene was wearing a petticoat on the night she disappeared, and the officers spotted traces of it on the bank below the newly found footprint. They theorized that this was the exact spot where the killer stopped his vehicle and rolled out Irene's lifeless body into the canal. The investigators couldn't collect the shoeprint because the mud was too watery due to the fact that it was raining outside for days. However, they did manage to determine that the killer wore men size 8 to 11.

The investigation intensified when Mayor Phillip Boeye encouraged the local police to work as hard as they could and that they shouldn't spare a single dollar because the town will cover the cost. The community wanted answers. Sure enough, the police broadened the investigation, interviewing more than 500 people in all of the surrounding towns near McAllen. They talked to Irene's family, her friends, and ex-boyfriends. Then they moved on to known criminals and sex offenders living in the area. But they still had no good lead to follow.

It was the beginning of May 1960 when the investigation took another turn. Many of the local police officers have heard the rumors about Father John Feit, and his name was constantly popping out during the interviews. He was twenty-seven years old at the time and arrived at McAllen after completing a seminary in San Antonio. Father John Feit planned to stay in McAllen for a year, hoping to become a pastor. While the parishioners liked his way of speaking and the fact that he was bilingual, Father John Feit did strike them as a bit strange. He was always by himself, rarely communicating with other pastors. On the other hand, numerous parishioners described him as polite and helpful.

But what made this young priest a person of interest to the McAllen police? The Sacred Heart Church was full during the Easter weekend, and numerous parishioners testified that Father John Feit was there, hearing confessions. He mentioned to Father Joseph O'Brien that he met with Irene Garza in the rectory on the night of her disappearance. Father O'Brien told this information to the police during his interview. He also mentioned that Father John Feit had some scratches on his hands when they saw each other after midnight for a cup of coffee. This contradicted Father John Feit's interview because he told the investigators that Irene came straight to the rectory, wishing to talk to him about a "question of conscience". He didn't provide any details but only mentioned that he sent Irene back to the church so she could confess there.

The previous attack

The detectives knew little about Father John Feit, but they started calling other departments, hoping that they had some information about the man. This was a smart move because Edinburg Police Department told them about the incident that happened only three weeks before Irene Garza's disappearance. Edinburg was one of Father John Feit's stops when he was driving from San Antonio to McAllen.

He visited the local Sacred Heart Church on March 23rd, 1960.

Maria America Guerra was in the church on the same day. She noticed a man parked in a blue and white car who was watching her go into the building. Several minutes after entering the church, the man was sitting in the back row by himself. Maria went to the altar in order to pray, and the man sneaked up on her, putting a rag over her mouth to stop her from screaming. Scared and startled, Maria fell to the ground, taking her attacker with her. The man still struggled to put his hand over Maria's mouth, and then she bit his fingers. Maria managed to get out of his grip and she ran outside, yelling for help.

The young woman was in shock, but she did manage to describe her attacker to the local authorities. She told them he had black rimmed glasses and dark hair. Even though he wasn't wearing his priest uniform, Maria remembered that he had black trousers on. They bore a resemblance to the ones worn by priests so she thought that her attacker might be a clergyman. She told this detail to the police, but she wasn't certain. As a devout Catholic, Maria felt guilty of accusing one of the priests of such a crime. Even though Edinburg police didn't catch her attacker, Maria's description was very helpful to the investigators from McAllen. The man she saw was very similar to Father John Feit.

Interviewing Father John Feit

Thinking that they might find some physical evidence of the murder at the bottom of the Second Street canal, the investigators ordered the divers to drag the section where they suspected the body was disposed of. They found an Eastman Kodaslide viewer right there in the mud. The viewer was photographed and published in the local newspapers, hoping that some of the residents might recognize it. Forty-eight hours later, the owner contacted the police department. The viewer belonged to Father John Feit who bought it almost one year ago. This was enough to bring the pastor in for questioning.

One thing that was suspicious to the investigators from the very beginning was the fact that the pastor had his whole timeline laid out perfectly. Father John Feit confirmed that he heard Irene's confession in the rectory which was completely against the rules, but he claimed that the young woman wanted some privacy. They left for church together sometime around 07:15 PM and that was apparently the last time Father John saw Irene. He spent the rest of his evening listening to the confessions, and he dropped by the rectory twice in order to have a break and smoke some cigarettes.

When questioned about the scratch marks mentioned by Father O'Brien, he had an answer ready. Father John Feit wore glasses and would often twirl them in his hands while listening to the confessions. He dropped a pair he was wearing that night. Father remembered that he had spare glasses in the pastoral house in San Juan, so he drove there that night. As soon as he parked in front, Father John Feit realized that he left the keys in McAllen. He didn't want to drive back and forth again, so he climbed on the second-floor balcony, entering the house through the double doors. Since he was climbing on a brick wall, he ended up with scratches on his right arm.

The interview continued on the next day, and the investigators questioned him about the attack on Maria America Guerra in Edinburg. Father John Feit confirmed that he was there on the day of the attack, but apparently, he left a couple of hours prior to the incident. He also mentioned that he was driving a blue and white car on that day, which fit Guerra's story. Father John Feit didn't want to stay long in Edinburg because he had to get back to San Juan in order to ring the bell. He hurt his finger on the same day, but his statement was that it got caught by a mimeograph machine.

The investigators suspected that Father John Feit was definitely hiding something. But without a crime scene, and any physical evidence connecting him to the murder, they knew that calling in for a reinforcement was a must. Polygraphs were a new technology, but they wanted to test it out on the priest. The detectives invited a team from Chicago to question Father John Feit. It took them two days of examination to determine that he was possibly involved in both incidents. The examiners were certain that he was not telling the truth about the murder of Irene Garza. He did pass the test, but some answers were inconclusive. The authorities were still skeptical about polygraphs, so this discovery led them nowhere.

As the time passed, the investigators worked less and less on solving the murder. Irene Garza's killing became a cold case because the detectives needed to tackle new crimes. The residents of McAllen still remembered the beautiful schoolteacher and would often mention her. Father John Feit did face a trial for the attack on Maria Guerra. He pleaded not guilty and ended up paying a $500 fine. The Catholic Church moved him to a monastery in 1963, hoping to cover up everything he had done in the past. Irene's parents died in the 1990s without getting any justice for the death of their daughter.

A new witness

In April of 2002, San Antonio police received a strange phone call. The caller's name was Dale Tachney, and he was a former priest who lived in a Trappist monastery in Missouri during the 1960s. The man claimed he had information about a murder that occurred on an Easter weekend in 1961 in San Antonio. Apparently, a fellow priest confessed to the crime while in a monastery. Detective George Saidler wrote down everything, but he was sure that the call itself was a fake. The caller described a gruesome murder to the finest details, telling him that a woman was tied up in a parish house. The priest now lived in Oklahoma City, and the detective had his contact number. He went through the database and saw that no murders occurred on that particular date in San Antonio.

At the same time, something big was happening in McAllen. Rudy Jaramillo, a Texas Ranger was appointed to open up the investigation of Irene Garza's death. His team was analyzing the cold cases hoping they could spot something other investigators missed. Even though he had boxes and boxes of files, nothing stood out to him. They even tested Irene's clothes for DNA since that technology was not available in the 1960s, and they found zero traces. Sheer luck connected Detective Saidler and Jaramillo. One Texas Ranger was visiting San Antonio police department and heard about the phone call they received. Even though the year didn't match up, the ranger remembered the case in McAllen that happened on an Easter weekend.

Rudy Jaramillo got the confession letter written by Dale Tacheny which was sent to Detective Saidler. The man was indeed a former monk who met Father John Feit in 1963. Tachney exited the church decades ago, but he felt guilty about the things he hid from the authorities. He wanted to provide Irene's family with a closure and put the murderer behind the bars. Tachney said the following: *I did not feel comfortable with the idea that I had in fact been a part of a cover-up, along with my abbot, of a priest that had committed murder.* The letter described everything he heard during the years he spent with Father John Feit. He was sent to Assumption Abbey by the Catholic Church in hopes the scandal would be avoided. After all, the United States was about to elect a Catholic president, and they needed to keep their image clean.

The details of the murder

Tachney was supposed to counsel Father John Feit and live with him during his stay at Assumption Abbey. The two became friends, and Tachney soon heard Father Feit's story. On the Saturday during the Easter weekend in 1960, Father John Feit invited Irene Garza to the rectory in order to hear her confession. He gagged her, and then tied the woman's hands behind her back. The priest proceeded to touch her breasts. Knowing that someone might notice his absence, Father Feit returned to the church, leaving Irene hidden in the basement.

When the morning came, Father John Feit took Irene to the second location. Tachney did not know where exactly. It is possible that he sexually assaulted Irene afterward. Aware that he had to get rid of the woman, he brought her to a bathtub and put a plastic bag on her head. Irene told him that she couldn't breathe, but the priest already knew that. He simply exited the room. He checked up on her several hours later and discovered that she suffocated. When the evening came, the priest carried Irene's body to his car, drove up to the canal, and dropped her body into the water. It is still unclear how his viewer ended up down there as well.

Tachney's recollection provided the investigators with almost all the answers they lacked in the case. Now they needed to locate Father John Feit. He left the church in 1972, after going through several programs for "troubled priests". It was obvious to him that he would not get another employment, so he decided to move on. The former priest started a family in Phoenix, Arizona, and worked as an insurance salesman. He was still very active in his local church.

The trials

The investigators managed to gather all of the necessary information in order to bring Father John Feit in front of a judge. Rene Guerra was a district attorney in Hidalgo County, but he was skeptical about the case. He decided to present it in a court in 2004, but the case was dismissed because Father O'Brien, who was one of the witnesses died that year. The trial was dropped, which disappointed the entire community. Rene Guerra held his position since the early 1980s, so district court judge Ricardo Rodriguez decided to try and get the seat in 2014. He promised the voters he would put Father John Feit on trial. Rodriguez became the district attorney and he kept his word.

Father John Feit was arrested in February of 2016 and was extradited to Texas two months later. He was eighty-three years old at the time and suffering from kidney and bladder cancer. He pleaded not guilty and judge Luis Singleterry placed a $1 million bond. The man waited for the trial in Hidalgo County Jail. Feit's defense tried to move the trial to another county, and this delayed the proceedings for months. After two jury selections and constant new dates, Father John Feit appeared in front of a judge on November 28th, 2017.

The trial itself moved fast, and he was found guilty on December 7th, 2017. Tachney was a star witness, and his testimony confirmed that the Catholic Church was behind the cover-up. One day later, the jury sentenced Father John Feit to life in prison for the murder of Irene Garza. Michael Garza, who was leading the prosecution asked for a sentence of 57 years, which is the exact time that passed since Irene was killed. He later said: *"All the cases like this you do expect that there will be an appeal. The judge was great on his rulings and I think we're solid."*

THE MURDER OF SISTER MARGARET ANN PAHL

Before the satanic panic of the mid-80s and the accusations of the sexual abuse within the institution, the Catholic Church managed to cover up a murder in Toledo, Ohio. It shouldn't come as a surprise because they were a very powerful organization back in the day and would do anything to save their reputation, including manipulation. The murder victim was a nun, and the only suspect – a priest.

Knowing how the public would react if this got out to the media, the higher-ups from the Catholic Church stopped the investigation completely, removing the accused from the area. However, it took a single letter from 2003 for this case to be re-examined in a new light. And after more than two decades later, the justice was finally served.

Margaret Ann Pahl's early life

Margaret Ann Pahl was born on April 6th, 1909 in a highly religious family. She wanted to become a nurse from an early age, so she studied medicine prior to her decision to become a nun. Margaret joined the Sisters of Mercy when she was only nineteen years old. The Sisters of Mercy is a well-known religious institute created in Ireland, but it quickly spread out throughout the globe. She put her medical knowledge to use and soon became a registered nurse, as well as a nun who dedicated her life to helping those in need.

As the time went by, Sister Margaret Ann Pahl continued her work at the Mercy Hospital in Toledo, Ohio. She was there to consult the younger members of the Sisters of Mercy, and show them the basics. Sister Margaret Ann Pahl was known for her strictness and perfectionism. She didn't hesitate to tell everyone what she really thinks and was very outspoken. Since Mercy Hospital had a chapel,

Margaret did her best to keep it in order. She would wake up every morning at 05:00 AM, and start her duties. There were more than twenty nuns at the hospital, and all of them were there to learn from Sister Margaret Ann Pahl.

Besides the nuns, there were also two priests living at the hospital. Their names were Father Gerald Robinson and Father Jerome Swiatecki. They were there to take care of the sick patients and those who are terminally ill. However, Sister Margaret Ann Pahl wasn't keen on Father Gerald Robinson. The two of them quarreled a lot during the time they spent together working at the hospital. As a matter of fact, the majority of the staff, as well as the nuns were familiar with the fact that Margaret Ann Pahl disliked Father Robinson.

Gerald Robinson also came from a religious family, and his mother was the one who made her son become a clergyman. He was born in Toledo, Ohio and stayed in his hometown for the entirety of his life. His mother financed Gerald's religious schooling from an early age, and he entered the priesthood when he was twenty-six years old. Catholic Church decided to keep him in Toledo to work in a hospital alongside Sister Margaret Ann Pahl. Their personalities simply clashed because Robinson mostly kept to himself, and Sister Margaret thought that he wasn't doing a good job. But he was still loved by the parishioners because he was fluent in Polish and Toledo had a large Eastern European community. So when the two of them got into a fight on April 4th, 1980 because he cut off his sermon early, and Sister Margaret Ann Pahl felt like he owed the parishioners to see it until the end because tomorrow was the Easter Sunday, nobody found it strange or out of the ordinary.

The discovery of the body

It was April 5th, 1980 when one of the nuns opened the doors to the chapel in order to start the early preparations for the Easter Sunday.

The hospital expected that the chapel will be completely filled because Easter Sunday is one of the biggest celebrations among Catholics. But as soon as she entered the room, the nun saw a shocking image in front of her. Margaret Ann Pahl's body was laying in the middle of the chapel. The woman was stabbed, and it was clear that something violent has happened during the night. The nun ran outside in a state of panic. She was searching for the phone to call the authorities.

When the investigators arrived at the scene, they were appalled by the viciousness of the murder. The nun was first strangled from behind and then laid down on the floor, where the killer continued to inflict her stab wounds all over her body. The wounds were mostly around her face, on the neck, and torso. However, the killer took the altar cloth and placed it over Sister Margaret Ann's chest before they stabbed her. When the police lifted the cloth off her body, they noticed that the stabs formed an inverted cross. This was a clear indication they were dealing with someone deranged and insane. They weren't sure if the murder had anything to do with Satanism, but everything pointed in that direction. Sister Margaret Ann Pahl also had a bloody cross drawn on her forehead which suggested that the last rite ceremony was performed on her body. In the end, the examiners counted a total of thirty-one stab wounds on Sister Margaret Ann Pahl.

Another detail that was shocking to the investigators was the fact that Margaret Ann's skirt was pulled up, exposing her lower body. The killer also took off her underwear, leaving it around her ankles. However, they couldn't determine if the nun was sexually assaulted because the murder scene looked very clean. It left them wondering if everything was staged to make it appear like the woman was also raped before or after the murder. Since it was the early 1980s and the DNA technology was not fully developed, the investigators had troubles finding any physical evidence on Sister Margaret Ann, or around her body.

The initial investigation

Once they analyzed the scene, the detectives started interviewing everyone in the hospital at the time. They first talked to the nuns who were also deeply disturbed about everything that happened. The majority of them mentioned Father Gerald Robinson and his relationship with Sister Margaret Ann. There were obvious tensions between the two of them, and the nuns thought that he might be involved in a way. However, they weren't sure if he was the killer because he was very withdrawn and quiet. It was hard to imagine that he could hurt anyone.

The entire hospital was searched because the investigators believed that the perpetrator was still there, hiding in plain sight. They went into each room occupied by the nuns and the priests. The detectives found an interesting item in Father Gerald Robinson's accommodation. It was a letter opener that resembled a small dagger. The blade could have been the one which was used to inflict the wounds found on Sister Margaret Ann Pahl's body. Knowing that the two of them argued on the day before the murder, the detectives were fairly certain that they had their suspect. But the letter opener was completely clean, just like the murder scene, and there were no visible traces of blood on it. However, a further analysis showed that there was some DNA material at the bottom of the blade. Unfortunately, it wasn't enough to run the full test in order to determine if it belonged to the murder victim or the killer.

Things were moving fast at the chapel, and the funeral for Sister Margaret Ann Pahl was held on April 8th, 1980. Since Margaret Ann didn't have many relatives in the area, the attendees were the nuns and priests from the hospital. Father Gerald Robinson wasn't officially accused of the killing, and he was not taken into the custody. He was allowed to lead the service for the murdered woman. Father Swiatecki was also there, and he also added a couple of sentences during the funeral.

With only one possible suspect, the police brought Father Gerald Robinson to the police station two weeks after the crime occurred. They wanted to conduct an official interview and hear what he had to say about the night when Sister Margaret Ann was killed. However, before the interview actually started, a monsignor appeared in the police station, and he led Father Robinson out. Soon enough, Father Robinson was transferred from the Mercy Hospital in order to become a pastor. He stayed in the area and was in charge of three parishes in Toledo. He continued to live and work like nothing happened. It was obvious to the detectives who were on this case that something was wrong. But they had no physical evidence that could connect the priest with the murder. And with that, the murder of Sister Margaret Ann Pahl became a cold case.

The cover-ups weren't unusual for the Catholic Church back in the days. They were still very powerful in the 1980s and were capable of hiding their own scandals. If something bad happened within the church, the high-ranking clergymen would intervene almost immediately. They had a developed system that would hide the crimes from the authorities. So the fact that they moved Father Robinson to a different parish wasn't strange at all. This was the best way to conceal the crime and influence the investigators to stop digging deeper. But the 1990s changed everything because the public became familiar with the sexual abuse within the church itself. The witnesses started coming forward, and soon enough, the investigators throughout the United States had more evidence about cold cases that were dormant for decades.

A new witness

The files about the murder of Sister Margaret Ann Pahl laid untouched for a total of twenty-three years. With no new leads or witnesses, the investigators were sure that the case will remain unsolved. It seemed like nobody was willing to talk. But everything changed in 2003 when one witness came forward. As previously mentioned, many women and children started speaking with the authorities about the abuse they suffered from the Catholic priests. An anonymous female sent a letter to Toledo Police Department in 2003. In it, she claimed that she went through a process of recovering her own memories and that she discovered she was a part of the satanic rituals performed by the Catholic priests when she was just a young girl. Since the experience was highly traumatic, her own mind managed to conceal it.

Probably the most interesting part of that letter was that she identified one of the priests involved in the satanic rituals. His name was Father Gerald Robinson. The detectives in Toledo knew the man well. They remembered he was the prime suspect in the murder of Sister Margaret Ann Pahl. The details of that case were very similar to the satanic rituals. After all, the nun was found with the stab wounds that formed an inverted cross. The anonymous woman who sent the letter to the police also mentioned that the priests involved in these rituals performed human sacrifice. Taking everything into the consideration, the investigators decided to open up the case once again in hopes that they missed something which could connect Father Gerald Robinson to the killing of Sister Margaret Ann Pahl.

The woman who sent the letter used the name Survivor Doe to file a civil lawsuit. She claimed that Father Gerald Robinson sexually abused her during the satanic rituals he performed. Survivor Doe said that there were other adults present in the room and she urged them to come out and testify on her behalf. She was unable to identify them on her own because they were wearing nun uniforms and their faces have been covered. Unfortunately, the case itself went nowhere due to the lack of evidence. It was finally dismissed in 2011 and Father Gerald Robinson wasn't charged with the sexual abuse of a minor. But Toledo Police Department started working hard on the case as soon as they received Survivor Doe's letter. New detectives were examining the physical evidence, and they had the technology that would give them better answers.

The re-opening of the case

The arrival of Survivor Doe's letter encouraged the investigators to re-examine the evidence that was collected at the crime scene. This also included the letter opener previously owned by Father Gerald Robinson. The letter opener looked like a small sword or a dagger. Even though the detectives who worked on the case in 1980 suspected that it might be the murder weapon, they never conducted a thorough examination. Toledo Police Department asked for the nun's body to be exhumed, and they sent it to the forensic unit alongside with the letter opener. They determined that one of the facial wounds was very likely inflicted with the letter opener because the blade was an almost perfect fit. However, they couldn't say that the blade was indeed the murder weapon.

After going through the interviews which were conducted immediately after the murder, the detectives noticed that several nuns who were working with Sister Margaret Ann Pahl mentioned that the woman always had a pair of scissors with her. They weren't found in her possession, or anywhere near the murder scene, which led the investigators to believe that the scissors might have been the murder weapon all along. Someone clearly picked them up and hid them from the police. They tested the stab wounds on Sister Margaret Ann's exhumed body and confirmed that scissors might have been the murder weapon as well.

Finally, the forensic unit took the swabs from underneath Sister Margaret Ann's fingernails, as well as from the inside of her underwear. The DNA technology wasn't as advanced in the 1980s but now they could test it in order to find the suspect. Sure enough, the swabs revealed that there was a presence of a male DNA under the nails and in her underwear. But it wasn't a match to Father Gerald Robinson. It belonged to a second person which led the investigators to suspect that there was more than one killer present at the chapel that night.

Since the investigators already had a list of people who were interviewed by the police back in 1980, they decided it might be time to talk to then again. They spoke with everyone they could locate and this led to the discovery of the brand new evidence which wasn't documented more than two decades ago. The police now had witnesses that were able to place Father Gerald Robinson near the crime scene around the time of the murder. It is still unclear why the witnesses failed to mention this detail during the initial investigation, but this allowed the detectives to start building the case against Father Robinson. He was near the chapel when Sister Margaret Ann Pahl was murdered and was in possession of the possible murder weapon.

Then they proceeded to interview Father Robinson himself who willingly went to the police station and gave them his own recollection of the murder. Father Robinson said that he was taking a shower when a nun entered his room in order to inform him that Sister Margaret was found dead in the chapel. He dressed in a hurry and went to the crime scene to see what was happening. When questioned about the murder back in 1980, Father Robinson said something very curious to the investigators. He told them that a man confessed to him that he murdered Sister Margaret Ann, but the priest had no authority to disclose the man's name. However, when asked to confirm this statement in 2004, Father Robinson claimed that he made the story up. Surely, they weren't able to produce a good motive for the murder, but the detectives hoped that Father Robinson would finally start telling the truth about the events that occurred on the night before the Easter Sunday back in 1980.

The arrest and the trial

On April 23rd, 2004 the investigators Tom Ross and Sargent Steve Forrester arrested Father Gerald Robinson for the murder of Sister Margaret Ann Pahl. They picked him up at his home in Toledo, Ohio. He was still working as a priest at the time of his arrest. He pleaded not guilty on May 7th, 2004. Father Robinson was set to wait for the trial out of the jail because his family managed to pay a $400,000 bond. Also, the church placed him on leave which meant that he was not allowed to perform any religious ceremonies during this time. The accusations were shocking to some of the parishioners who knew Father Gerald Robinson for years. As a matter of fact, he gathered a huge following who supported the claims of his innocence. One parishioner called Jack Sparagowski started collecting money that would pay off the defense fees for Father Robinson. He raised a total of $12,000. When asked why he believed in Father Robinson's innocence, Sparagowski told the following: *"For someone to commit murder, you have to have a violent streak. I've never heard Father raise his voice or show any expression of anger. The whole thing seems so bizarre."*

The investigators working on this cold case were not sure if they should mention the satanic part of the murder. Dave Davison who was the first police officer on the scene stood firm with his beliefs that the whole ritualistic setup of the murder was actually another cover-up which was supposed to steer the investigation into a wrong direction. Prior to the trial, Ross and Forrester invited Dawn Perlmutter who is an expert in ritualistic killings, to hear her own take on the murder. Having in mind that Survivor Doe spoke about satanic rituals in her letter, the prosecution was willing to mention this part during the trial. However, Perlmutter advised them to avoid the narrative because the public is not eager to accept that these things actually do happen and that they might have a hard time convincing the jury.

The trial began on April 17th, 2006 in a Lucas County courtroom. The judge was Thomas Osowik, and he handled numerous high-profile cases in Toledo, Ohio. The media covered the trial thoroughly, and it quickly became one of the most interesting events in Ohio that year. However, there was also some backlash from the public, namely the members of the community who believed that the police was once again covering up the grisly details of the sexual abuse in the Catholic Church. Claudia Vercelloti who is a director of Survivors Network of those Abused by Priests in Toledo, criticized the authorities for focusing their investigation on the murder only. She was positive that there was more to it, and that the sexual abuse described in Survivor Doe's letter needed to be tied in with the killing as well. After all, Survivor Doe named Father Gerald Robinson as one of the abusers. Vercelloti said the following: *We know this is a trial about murder, but the cover-up can't be ignored.*

Dean Mandros was appointed as the lead prosecutor, and Chris Anderson was chosen as a part of the team. Both of them were very successful in the past and confident that they could win this case as well, even though they only had circumstantial evidence. Father Robinson found excellent defense layers - Alan Konop and John Thebes. The trial began after the jury selection, and the first to testify was Sister Phyllis Ann Gerold. She was the one who saw Father Gerald Robinson near the scene of the crime at the time the murder was committed. Sister Gerold confirmed that Father Robinson was not in his room and that he was on the floor where the chapel was located.

Even though the prosecution was advised not to mention the ritualistic murders during the trial, they invited Father Jeffrey Grob as one of their witnesses. Father Grob is an expert when it comes to analyzing different rituals. While he avoided connecting the murder to Satanism, he did mention that a priest would have enough knowledge to stage the murder scene and make it appear like a ritual was performed on the body of the victim. He wasn't able to confirm that

Sister Margaret Ann Pahl was killed during the ritual itself, but Father Grob said that an inverted cross was a very common symbol in Satanism.

The prosecution managed to recruit a famous forensic investigator Dr. Henry Lee who was a part of several prominent cases including the murder of JonBenet Ramsey and the O.J. Simpson trial. Dr. Henry Lee was there to give his assessment of the possible murder weapon, as well as to determine if the crime scene was staged. While he confirmed that the letter opener which was found in Father Robinson's possession could have been the blade which was used to kill Sister Margaret Ann Pahl, he was uncertain about the imprints on the altar cloth. One bloody trace was very similar to the decorations found on the handle of the letter opener. Dr. Henry Lee could not dismiss the claims that the murder scene was staged in order to look like a sexual assault, as well as a satanic ritual.

The defense called Dr. Kathy Reichs, a well-known forensic anthropologist to give her own evaluations of the wounds found on Sister Margaret Ann Pahl's exhumed body. Dr. Reichs said that the findings were inconclusive and she suspected that another weapon was used to kill Sister Pahl. However, she couldn't rule out the possibility either. Dr. Reichs mentioned that the scissors owned by Sister Margaret Ann Pahl were a more believable murder weapon. She came to this conclusion after examining the images of the stab wounds provided to her by the defense.

Father Gerald Robinson stayed silent during the trial. He never spoke to anyone and refused to testify on his behalf. His defense lawyers argued that the prosecution had no physical evidence tying their defendant to the murder. Everything they presented was circumstantial, including the letter opener. Not to forget that an unknown male DNA was discovered at the scene as well. The defense also stated that Father Robinson didn't have any motive for the murder which sparked a heated discussion about the fact that Father Robinson argued with Sister Pahl one day before the killing.

The verdict and aftermath

The jury retreated to discuss the case on May 11th, 2006. It took them only six hours of deliberation to reach the verdict. Father Robinson sat in the courtroom, wearing his clerical collar, looking calm and composed. The jury found him guilty of the murder of Sister Margaret Ann Pahl. The judge sentenced him to fifteen years to life, with the possibility of a parole after ten and a half years. Father Robinson refused to comment on the ruling, not breaking his silence throughout the whole procedure. He was escorted to Lucas County jail.

As the prosecution exited the courtroom, they were cheered by the people waiting for the sentencing. Dean Mandros, the lead prosecutor made a comment immediately after leaving the court in which he said: *"I don't see it as a reason to celebrate. We're dealing with a homicide case. We're trying to hold the person responsible accountable. We didn't go back in the office and high-five each other."* Mandros also mentioned that he was certain Father Robinson murdered Sister Margaret Ann Pahl in a fit of blind rage. When asked about the ritualistic part of the murder, he dismissed it. Instead, Mandros said: *"Perhaps the most common scenario there is for a homicide: A man got very angry at a woman and the woman died. The only thing different is that the man wore a white collar and the woman wore a habit."*

Father Gerald Robinson suffered a heart attack in May of 2014. He died on July 4th, 2014 in Franklin Medical Center in Columbus, Ohio where he was imprisoned. Father Robinson became a first known Catholic priest in the United States who was found guilty of murdering a nun.

THE MURDER OF SISTER CATHY

Accounts of an abusive Catholic priest, a nun questioning her vows, a missing girl reported to the Church rather than the police. A body chewed to nothing by wildlife. A second murder, with links to the first. Nearly forty years after her death, police in Baltimore are no closer to finding the culprit in the disturbing case of Catherine Cesnik than they were back in 1969.

Was she simply the victim of a robbery gone wrong? Had she been sexually assaulted, then killed, her body left to rot on the wastelands of the most run-down part of the city? Or was the case connected with a priest, later accused of crimes against the young, whose actions were about to be revealed?

Sister Catherine, Cathy as she was known, was a teaching nun, one who had found her vocation in life early on. Born in Lawrenceville, Pittsburgh, Pennsylvania, she was the daughter of East European immigrants. Her paternal grandparents had emigrated to Pittsburgh from what is now Slovenia, while on her mother's side, her grandparents had originated in Yugoslavia and Austria. There were four children in the family, and Cathy was the eldest.

She was a good girl, helpful around the house and to her parents, and the family were close. Indeed, at her funeral many years later, her father was inconsolable. Cathy attended local Catholic schools and was frequently inspired by the nuns who taught her. She was intensely religious as a girl and had pretty much decided that a life dedicated to the Church was the path she wanted to follow. Such beliefs were firmed up at St Augustine Catholic High School, which she entered in 1956. During her successful time there, she was both May Queen and Valedictorian in her graduation year.

A Vocation

In 1960, she left school and entered the Notre Dame convent with the intention of becoming a School Sister (the name given to nuns who were also teachers). Like all those new to an abbey, her time began as a postulant, a kind of nun in training. Later, on its release, a film about a heroic, life changing postulant would become her own inspiration. She was fascinated by 'The Sound of Music', whose heroine, Maria, helps an Austrian family to escape the rise of the Nazis, falling in love herself into the bargain. But that was still to come, the Baltimore Province Convent of the School Sisters of the Notre Dame welcomed her, and the next seven years of her life were committed to advancing from postulant status. She took her final vows in the summer of 1967.

It is hard to think of a more impressive young lady. At a time when her peers were embracing hippy-hood, the drugs culture and opposing everything for which their parents stood, young Cathy was a model of respectability. Certainly, there was a lot to oppose in the 1960s, not least the war in Vietnam, and later in the decade the corrupt Government of the Nixon era, but Cathy wanted none of that. To her, a life devoted to God and her students was all she desired. In fact, she began teaching in 1965, working as a drama and English teacher in the Archbishop Keough High School in South west Baltimore, a new school built to address the problems of poor education in the area.

It was a challenging enough place for a young lady. Catering for the largely Irish American community living locally, it was located in a working class, run down area of the city. Many of the students entered school behind in their studies and with the associated problems of poverty.

But Catherine Cesnik was a model teacher, just as she seemed a perfect representative of the Catholic Church. She transformed a high percentage of her students, assisting many out of poverty. Gemma Hoskins was a case in point. Her subsequent thirty-year teaching career was inspired by time under the tutelage of Sister Cathy. Hoskins was even awarded 'Maryland Teacher of the Year', back in 1992. 'Catherine Cesnik is the reason I became a teacher. I still regard her as the finest teacher I ever had,' said the former educator a few years ago.

She was not alone in her praise for Cesnik. After her death, many of her current and former students came forward with heartfelt compliments. 'Outstanding.' 'Our Pied Piper,' and 'the kind of teacher you never forget,' were comments typically laid at the door of the tragic teacher.

Branching Out

But, sometime in 1968 or '69 things began to change for Cathy. She still loved her teaching, but she started to become distracted. Was she beginning to regret her decision to commit to a life of devotion...and chastity? This was a young lady, still in her mid-twenties, who had really known nothing outside a life of religious commitment. From her childhood, her love of God – a Catholic God – informed all she did. Had she begun to crave something more? Another former student, who wanted to remain nameless, spoke to journalist Tom Nugent, author of the definitive account of the demise of Catherine Cesnik.

'To me, she seemed stressed out, perhaps even on the edge of a nervous breakdown,' the former student claimed. 'She was exhausted and extremely nervous, and she missed a lot of school during the spring months.'

Then, in June of 1969, Cathy made an unusual, but not unheard of, request to those in authority at the Notre Dame. She requested to enter a period of exclaustration. This is basically a time of experimentation whereby a nun takes a temporary break from living in the cloistered environment of the abbey. Instead, while in no way abandoning her beliefs, the nun moves into outside accommodation. She also abandons the traditional habit and instead is able to wear the normal dress of the times – skirt, blouse and so forth. With good sense, those in authority granted her wish, sensing that after a short time in the 'outside' world, Cathy's need for experimentation would pass. She would begin to see the corruption and unkindness of life in the harshest streets of Baltimore. In time, she would return to the abbey, a wiser, experienced and worldlier lady, with a stronger then ever commitment to her life's mission.

But soon, Cathy needed even more than exclaustration. She decided that she would take a temporary break from the Keogh School, and instead enrolled to teach at a tough public school, called Western High. There, she would serve as a missionary teacher.

On leaving the abbey, she moved into a two-bedroomed apartment in the Carriage House, on North Bend Road in the city. She shared her new flat with another nun, Sister Helen Russell Phillips, who also had embarked on a period living in the outside world. The two were great friends and held open house for many of Cathy's former students. Several became friends with Sister Helen as well, often helping out with sewing and other tasks.

But why would a seemingly happy School Sister, who had spent a life of devotion to her beliefs, suddenly want to experience such changes in her life? Certainly, it could be that she simply wanted to see more of the world, to find out what it was to live like a normal twenty something in the swinging sixties, without the impact of a black and white habit to change people's reaction to her.

That would be understandable. But two other, less palatable, possibilities began to emerge following the violent and untimely death that was soon to occur. Each involved a Catholic priest, and the alleged behaviour of those priests, to different degrees, was unacceptable within the church. Were their 'crimes', physical and criminal respectively, something that the Church could simply not allow to become public, at whatever cost?

The Facts Of The Case

With no perpetrator ever arrested, police still occasionally re visit the murder of Catherine Cesnik, although with ever less frequency these days. All that they have to work on now are bare facts. On November 7th 1969, Cathy left her Baltimore apartment in the late afternoon to do some shopping at the nearby centre, just half a mile away. She travelled by car, and was looking to buy some groceries for dinner, a present for her sister's imminent wedding and to get some cash. Edmondson Village Shopping Centre was somewhere with which she was already familiar, even though she had lived in her Westgate apartment for just a few months. She never returned. As early evening moved to night time, Helen Russell Phillips began to become increasingly worried about her friend's absence. Like her flatmate, Helen was an innocent girl, not used to making decisions on her own. After all, she had spent much of her adult life in the confines of the abbey, where most decisions were made for her. When a problem arose, the nuns sorted it. It was a protected, secure existence, but the down side was that inhabitants became partially institutionalised and lacked the capability to make decisions of their own.

What should Helen do? Eventually, she phoned a priest she knew was friendly with Cathy. By that time, it was already 11 p.m. but the Jesuit priest sensed the worry in her voice. He realised that for Cathy to be out at that time, without telling her friend to expect her home late, was out of character. While it was certainly the case that many women of her age, back in the late 1960s, might change their plans at the last moment if they met a girlfriend, or bumped into a man with whom they got talking, that was not something Cathy would do. The priest lived in a Jesuit community called Manresa, which was based near Annapolis. He got into his car and, taking along a colleague, set off on the thirty miles journey to the nuns' apartment.

He arrived with Brother Peter McKeon a short while later. It appears as though the three spent some time wondering what to do. No doubt debating whether it was, in fact, possible that Cathy was acting out of character, and they were worrying about nothing. In the end, sometime after midnight, they called the police and reported their friend as missing. Still anxious, they talked away into the night. At around four a.m., with still no sign of Cathy, they decided to calm their nerves by taking a walk in the bitter November air. It was then that, a short distance from the apartment block, they spied Cathy's car. The green Ford Maverick was parked up, but at an odd angle. It was as though the car had been returned but at the last moment the driver had panicked and left the vehicle just before completing the parking manoeuvre.

Detectives Harry Bannon and Tony Glover were put in charge of the case. They led the search for the missing young lady. But it was all to no avail. The community was scared at the thought of a potential attacker in their midst. It was shocked that the missing woman was a nun. Her good nature and commitment to her vocation, both as a teacher and as a religious figure, made her a popular person. Her students and colleagues adored her. Those in her neighbourhood who had begun to get to know the quiet, smiling nun – one who always had a pleasant word and a cheery face – were horrified about what might have happened to her.

A Body Is Found

November passed, then December, Christmas and the New Year. But on January 3rd 1970 a couple of hunters were making their way out to the woods for some shooting when they passed a garbage dump in the isolated community of Lansdowne, in the southwest of Baltimore County. There, they saw something that caught their attention, something that only barely resembled a human. It was the animal savaged remains of an adult female. The hunters informed the police, and the local station contacted the murder squad. Within a few moments, the call made its way to Captain 'Bud' Roemer, commander of 'M Squad.'

Roemer was involved in the investigation of well over a hundred murder enquiries during his working life, many were solved, some not. The case of Sister Catherine Cesnik, though, made a greater impact on him than most. 'Every homicide cop has one case that haunts him to the end of his career,' he said shortly before his death in the 2000s. 'And

Sister Cathy is mine. I sure do wish we could close this one out, before I kick the bucket.' His wish would not be satisfied.

Roemer got together his team, and they set off for the Halethorpe Precinct where the body had been found. It began to snow as the officers clambered into their unmarked Plymouths, the black shapes making their way carefully through the cold, contrasting sharply with the white ground beneath them.

They walked up the dump and, having assisted local police in the search for the missing nun, Roemer had little doubt with whom he was confronted. 'Hello, Cathy Cesnik' he murmured to the lonely body.

The identity was quickly confirmed. Cathy was lying on her back, half way up a small slope. One shoe had come off and lay a short distance away. Her purse was also nearby, and inside resting a bottle of medication. Her name was printed on it.

When a murder occurred, the officers knew they were in for long days, for many frustrations and lost leads as they investigated. First steps were to follow the guidelines. An autopsy was ordered for as soon as possible, and on that bitterly cold, snow covered, and reeking garbage dump officers spent four, maybe five, hours searching for clues.

'She'd been laying out on the dump all this time, and the varmints had gotten to her,' Roemer told Tom Nugent in an interview thirty-five years after her murder. The images were vivid in the old, former detective's mind. They had been scorched into his memory. There was something even more wrong in the juxta position between a beautiful and innocent young nun and the corruption with which the officers were now faced.

So badly had her body been molested by the wildlife in those two months she had lain, exposed, on the dump, that it was impossible to tell whether the attack had been sexually motivated. Indeed, that is something that will never be known unless the murderer is ever caught. The autopsy report provided by the medical examiner confirmed that it was impossible to tell whether she had been molested. And as for the murderer, he or she must now be in their seventies, eighties or nineties. Quite probably they too are dead, their murky secret with them in the grave.

Another officer to see Cathy's body that day on the dump was James Scannell. He would go on to become a Captain in the Baltimore County Police, before retiring. The impact on him was, as with Roemer, considerable.

'I remember her blue coat, and the purse nearby,' he recalled during an interview in 2004.

There would follow a five-year investigation into the murder. It was a barren half a decade, a journey of numerous dead ends and false leads that ultimately ended in nothing. Subsequent follow up investigations, including some by the FBI, also failed to reveal the truth.

But back to the two priests, and their behaviour that caused the authorities serious concerns. One of these would, in years to come, throw the Church into one of its far too many crises.

A Matter of Love

The first matter involved Father Koob, the priest who had made the cross-town journey to Cathy's apartment on the day she went missing. It must be said that Koob was never a serious suspect in the case. He was quickly found to have a watertight alibi for that evening. He had shared dinner with friends, and then spent the evening watching 'Easy Rider' on TV, along with another priest.

But something about Koob didn't quite ring true with Bud Koemer. He felt that there was something more, something about the priest's reactions which caused a tremor of concern. The police decided to put pressure on the man, and he admitted a closeness between himself and Cathy, but one that was purely platonic. For a man of the Catholic cloth, there could be no more.

Yet there had to be a reason why Helen Russell had phoned the priest, rather than the police, when she first realised that something was wrong. Many hours of interrogation followed – not because Koob was a suspect in the crime, but because the police felt he knew something that might put the events of the previous November into some kind of perspective.

At one point, they visited Father Koob's home at the Mansera Jesuit community. There, the priest handed over a letter he had received shortly after Cathy's disappearance. It was all the more distressing that had posted it prior to her abduction and murder. Perhaps she even sent it from a post-box at the shopping centre on the day of her death. Koob had not mentioned the letter before, according to the authorities, but now he wished to do all he could to assist with their enquiries.

The letter implied that the relationship between the two had been somewhat stronger than had been suggested:

'My Dearest Gerry,

"If Ever I Should Leave You" is playing on the radio. I'm all curled up in bed. My 'period' has finally arrived, ten days late…so you might say I'm moody…my heart ache is for you.'

From the opening address, the letter included the kind of content that would hardly be expected between a nun and priest, however friendly they might have been. It went on:

'I must wait on you, your time and your need – even more than I had before.' Next, its words clearly indicated, from Cathy's perspective at least, that the life of celibacy required by the church was far from on her agenda.

'I must tell you, I want you within me, I want to have your children.'

Accounts differ as to what happened next. The police claim that Koob quickly broke down and admitted that the two young Catholics (Koob being just a year older than Cathy) had engaged in a sexual relationship. Of course, such a matter was not for the police to judge, nor did they do so, but it was something that would cause controversy if it emerged and would probably result in one or both of the couple being forced to abandon their vocation.

That, in itself, was cause for the investigators to reconsider their approach. They now had a possible reason for Cathy's wish to take time away from the abbey, to experience life in the real world. They also had reason to believe that the priest might know a little more about what happened that night than he was letting on.

Koob, on the other hand, always denied that he had been involved in any sexual relations with Cathy. Later, he did leave the Catholic Church. He married and became a Methodist Minister

For a while, police thought that they had a new lead, but it went nowhere. Yes, Koob and Cathy were friends, at the very least. But, Koob's alibi was completely watertight and, when they came to think about it, for Helen to phone a priest to come to her aid when Cathy went missing was perhaps not that inexplicable. Again, although the allegation is disputed, it seems as though the Church also put pressure on the police to lay off of Koob. This was denied by the Catholic hierarchy, but the Church's track record from that era makes any such denial neither here nor there. Koemer also said that this did not happen, and that he would have ignored it if it had, but investigator Harry Bannon, also on the case, argued the matter. 'The church lawyers stepped in and they talked to the higher-ups at the police department,' he claimed 'and we were told to either charge Koob with a crime or let him go. Stop harassing him.'

Any case against Koob was firmly buried.

Claims of Abuse

But there was a second priest against whom the police would hold serious suspicions. In this case, the breach with both Catholic and society's law was more severe, criminal indeed. And the evidence of Cathy's involvement was much greater.

A serious rumour was circulating at the Keough school. The Catholic Church's record in child abuse cases is about as bad as it could be. Not only has it been rife across the globe, but the Church's response has sometimes been to threaten, buy off and otherwise attempt to silence complainants, while simply shifting the alleged perpetrators to new posts in other areas. Maybe that was why at least four young girls visited their well-liked, respected and youthful teacher, Cathy Cesnik, to tell her that they too had fallen victim. But that revelation stayed secret until many years after Cathy's death. Then, in the mid-1990s, everything came out: a $40 million law suit was launched claiming that the Keogh school Chaplain, a Diocesan priest called Anthony Joseph Maskell, had committed widespread abuse against female students at the institution. Over thirty witnesses offered support to the case, alleging wide ranging abusive acts including vaginal and anal intercourse, sexual assault, oral sex, physical violence and enforced prostitution. It was claimed that the victims had, in some cases, been forced into sex acts with a police officer or officers.

Catholics and people of other religious persuasion where concerned, in Baltimore and beyond, by the accusations. It was then that it was first claimed, by no less than four women, that they had spoken to Cesnik about the matter. But if shock was the over-riding emotional response to the allegations against Maskell, then that would fall far from prominence in people's minds when one of the possible victims made an astonishing claim. In order to protect her identity at that time, this woman (one of the two behind the lawsuit) was named as Jane Doe. She said that in November 1969, she had been driven to a garbage dump in Lansdowne by Maskell. There, the priest had taken her to see a shocking sight – that of a dead woman. The reason? If Jane Doe said anything about the abuse she had suffered, she now knew what would happen to her.

Clearly, if her story was true, then Maskell would be in the frame as the chief suspect. Even if he had not been responsible for Cathy's murder, then he would at the very least know a lot about what had happened to the nun. Another victim claimed that Maskell had threatened her with a gun to stop her from going public about the abuse. Was Maskell an abuser? And was he so violent that he would stoop to murder to save his skin?

The case was dismissed.

A technical matter about the admissibility of 'recovered memory' meant that the matter was thrown out of court. Yet the evidence against Maskell appeared strong. The church itself conducted an internal enquiry, and Maskell had his 'faculties revoked'; in other words, he was removed from his then role, as a pastor of St. Augustine's parish Elkridge. What else could the Church do? Elkridge lies just ten miles from central Baltimore. Maskell needed moving for his own protection, guilty or not. Move he did, taking up a role as a child psychologist in Ireland where he would also occasionally lead Mass.

And this was the mid-1990s. At the time society still believed that people did not lie about abuse claims. That they did not make them up for money, for attention. That they did not hold mistaken memories. Whether Jane Doe (and her fellow claimant, 'Jane Roe') were victims or not we cannot know for certain. Their case was strong, but not strong enough. Maskell was found innocent. It was also the belief of his family and friends that he had been wrongly accused. Many in the police department felt the same way. The former director of personnel at the Maryland State Police was Jim Jones, a lieutenant colonel. He said of Maskell, who spent time as the Baltimore County Police Department Chaplain, that he did a 'terrific job.' Others were equally fulsome in their support – James Scannell, a former Police Captain said, 'He was a wonderful priest and a loyal friend.'

'Keepers' – Could Netflix Solve the Case?

Maskell died in 2001, but he would not be allowed to rest in peace. His body was dug up as the case regarding Cathy was revisited prior to a Netflix documentary called 'Keepers'. The series re-examined the murder, and Maskell's DNA was taken to see if he could be identified as having a link to the crime. There proved to be no match. Maskell's death seems to have been the cue for Janes Doe and Roe to go public; Jean Wehner and Teresa Lancaster allowed themselves to be identified and continued to fight their case. Lancaster alleged that her parents sent her to see the police after they found cannabis in her possession.

She alleged that the priest made her strip naked and sit on his lap. She says that he said he could help her more if she was naked; the abuse, she claimed continued for two years, up to three times per week.

Ultimately, the Baltimore Diocese has paid out close to half a million dollars to sixteen alleged victims of the priest. Matters are now being investigated in Ireland, where he may have continued to abuse the vulnerable.

Much of the content of the Netflix Cold Case documentary series came from the evidence of Whener and Lancaster (the latter two finding numerous alleged witnesses to Maskell's possible crimes). A police officer, Nick Giangrasso also featured, coming forward to say he had been taken off the case by the hierarchy, the investigation handed over to another department when he started to get close to a result. The documentary, though, has been criticised for its treatment of the case, many feeling Netflix sensationalised the event. Several possible other murderers are suggested during the series, which was released in 2017. These include both different priests and a police led paedophile ring which is alleged to have been in operation at the time. The claim is also made that Maskell, whose brother was a policeman, received special protection from both the police and the Church. Most of the programme's ire is indeed reserved for Maskell. Lancaster felt he could even have been a serial killer. Of his alleged abuse victims, she said: 'I am certain more will follow. There could be as many as 100 of his victims.'

Baltimore lawyer, Joanne Suder, represents many of the people who have claimed that they were abused. There is no doubt that she feels the Catholic Church has, just as with other abuse scandals, failed to be open. Evidence has been hidden. Suder is very much to the point. 'It's horrifying, the Catholic Church should be ashamed of itself,' she has said.

A Second Murder?

One final twist exists with this case. Just six days after Cathy went missing, another body was discovered in the area. Joyce Malecki was only twenty, and she was found stabbed and strangled to death, on the US military base at Fort Meade. It is another unsolved crime.

Many felt that there could be a connection between the two murders, although this was never proved. However, the Malecki family, who lived less than a mile from where Cathy's body was found, had close connections with the Keogh school, even if Joyce did not attend. She did, though, go along to holiday retreats run by Catholic priests. The church attended by the family, St Clement Church, was one at which Father Maskell from time to time worked.

The extent of the connection between the crimes should have been fully investigated, but something went wrong. Later it emerged that the FBI – in charge of the case because Joyce's body was found on Government land, thought it had passed over the matter to the local police. The local police thought the FBI had the case in hand. A simple error, or the interfering hands of an influential force?

Two murders: locations match, age groups match, links to the church match and links to Keogh school also exist. It seems too coincidental to ignore.

But time passes. The murder of Cathy Cesnik remains unsolved. Was her murderer an abusive priest who knew the area in which she was abandoned like the back of his hand? Was there some kind of conspiracy involving the church, and truths it wanted to stay hidden? Did Cathy Cesnik simply know too much to be allowed to live? Was she about to reveal accusations that would send the Maryland church, and some individuals, spinning out of control? Or was it simpler, a straightforward sex attack, or a robbery gone wrong. One in which the culprit kindly drove her car back to her home!

All that we know for sure is that Cathy was beaten to death on or shortly after that night in November 1969. A single blow to the head seems to have been the significant strike. One that left a small round hole, such as may have been made by a hammer, or an iron tool. Or perhaps a ring, which hit her head with such force from the killer's fist that it left a fatal wound. The sort of wound that might be caused by a ring such as the heavy gold kind worn on the fingers of some Catholic priests.

9 7 9 8 2 2 4 9 0 7 4 2 7